E. W

the
TWO
KINDS
of
Life

DISCOVER THE LOST TRUTH THAT
JESUS CAME TO GIVE US

WHITAKER
HOUSE

Unless otherwise indicated, all Scripture quotations are taken from the *New King James Version*, © 1982 by Thomas Nelson, Inc. Used by permission. All rights reserved. Scripture quotations marked (rsv) are taken from the *Revised Standard Version of the Bible*, © 1952 [2nd edition, 1971] by the Division of Christian Education of the National Council of Churches of Christ in the U.S.A. Used by permission. All rights reserved. Scripture quotations marked (wnt) are taken from *The New Testament in Modern Speech* by R. F. (Richard Francis) Weymouth. Scripture quotations marked (ylt) are taken from *Young's Literal Translation* by Robert Young (1898).

THE TWO KINDS OF LIFE
Discover the Lost Truth that Jesus Came to Give Us

Kenyon's Gospel Publishing Society
P.O. Box 973
Lynnwood, WA 98046-0973
www.kenyons.org

ISBN: 979-8-88769-342-2

Printed in the United States of America
© 2025 by Kenyon's Gospel Publishing Society

Whitaker House
1030 Hunt Valley Circle
New Kensington, PA 15068
www.whitakerhouse.com

Library of Congress Control Number: 2024946674

No part of this book may be reproduced or transmitted in any form or by any means, electronic or mechanical—including photocopying, recording, or by any information storage and retrieval system—without permission in writing from the publisher. Please direct your inquiries to permissionseditor@whitakerhouse.com.

1 2 3 4 5 6 7 8 9 10 11 Ⓤ 32 31 30 29 28 27 26 25

CONTENTS

First Words 5
A Definition 7
   1. A Biological Discovery 9
   2. The Greatest Biological Fact in Human Experience 15
   3. The Need of Eternal Life 23
   4. Manner of Life 31
   5. Recreation of the Human Spirit 34
   6. Spiritual Death 42
   7. What Eternal Life Does 44
   8. Spiritual Forces 50
   9. Some Eternal Life Realities 54
   10. Eternal Life Gives Love 64
   11. When Was Eternal Life First Given to Man? 69
   12. The Reign of Eternal Life 72
   13. Right and Wrong Confessions 79

14. The Renewed Mind	90
15. Men of the Senses Versus Men of the Spirit	97
16. I Am What God Says I Am	104
17. Walking in the Light of Life	109
18. All the Words of This Life	113
19. The New Man	116
20. The Father-God Consciousness	123
21. Cultivating Our Own Spirits	126
22. Developing the Human Spirit	133
23. Spiritual Growth	140
24. The Lordship of Jesus	147
25. The Great Spiritual Forces in the World	150
26. The Reality of the Word	162
27. What We Are in Christ	165
28. Some Mighty Facts	174
29. What Is the Matter?	183
30. The Unbelieving Believer	187
31. A New Type of Christianity	197
About the Author	208

FIRST WORDS

The whole human race is facing a new era. Civilization is in a state of flux. Sense knowledge has failed again. It has destroyed what revelation knowledge has accomplished in the last four centuries.

Sense knowledge has never produced a civilization that it did not destroy, nor given a monetary system that did not enslave the masses, nor originated an educational system that did not corrupt the spirit of youth.

Sense knowledge has gained the supremacy over Christianity and dominates it.

The mass of humanity has lost God and knows not how to find Him.

Civilization has failed because the type of Christianity we have given it has failed. It was a sense-ruled type that was stripped of miracles.

We believe that this book has the solution to the individual problem, the national problem, and the world problem.

This is not a new philosophy. It is an unveiling of a lost truth, the most vital of all that God gave to us in Christ.

Please read this with tolerance, yet with an open mind. It has the solution to the problems which the church is facing today.

A DEFINITION

Eternal life is the nature of God. Jesus gave us the first intimation of what this life would do for man.

In Him was life, and the life was the light of men. (John 1:4)

The Greek word is *zoe*, the new kind of life that Jesus brought to the world. In John 10:10, He said, *"I have come that they may have life [zoe], and that they may have it more abundantly."*

Man was to have a right to enjoy an abundance of a new kind of life.

There are four Greek words translated "life" or "manner of life" in the New Testament. The first one is *psuche*, which means "natural, human life." The second is *bios*, which means "manner of life, customs." The third is *anastrophee*, which is used seven or more times in the New Testament, means "a confused behavior."

It is a strange thing that the church has majored *manner of life* or *behavior* rather than eternal life, which determines in a very large way the manner of life.

Receiving eternal life is the most miraculous incident or event in life. It is called conversion, the new birth, and the new creation. Some have called it *getting religion*, but it is, in reality, God imparting His very nature, substance, and being to our human spirits.

Paul describes it this way:

Therefore, if anyone is in Christ, he is a new creation; old things have passed away; behold, all things have become new. Now all things are of God, who has reconciled us to Himself through Jesus Christ, and has given us the ministry of reconciliation. (2 Corinthians 5:17–18)

This is a miraculous recreation of man. It is God actually giving birth to a new man.

The new creation, then, is a miracle thing. It is man receiving a foreign nature that recreates his spirit and makes him a new species among men.

The church has never majored in this new creation fact. Its leaders have never realized the possibilities that this new nature offers to men.

None of the old religions of the world have ever changed the nature of their followers. They did not impart to man a new element.

Christianity gives to man God's very own nature.

1

A BIOLOGICAL DISCOVERY

Biology is the study of life in all of its varied forms and manifestations. It knows much about mineral life, metal life, vegetable life, animal life, and human life.

But another life, the mother of all life, has been ignored by both scientists and modern thinkers. Its effect upon humanity is one of the miracles of human experience.

Jesus promised it in John 10:10: *"I have come that they may have life, and that they may have it more abundantly."*

CONTRAST OF TWO WORDS

There are two Greek words that are translated "life." One is *psuche*, which means natural, human life; and the other is *zoe*, which is eternal life or God's life.

This new kind of life is God's nature. It is called eternal life in the Word. This life produces certain changes in man. People can see the effect of this life at once in a man—in his habits, his speech. It changes conduct, corrects habits, and forms new ones.

The people who have it are known as the *twice-born men*, the new creation men.

Its effect on the lives, habits, and qualities of people is often amazing. Boys and girls who receive it in their teens seldom, if ever, sow wild oats.

There are no child criminals who have it. No girls in houses of prostitution have it. No drunkards have it. No confirmed cigarette users have it. No criminals have it. No crooks or thieves or crooked politicians have it.

First John 3:15 says, "*You know that no murderer has eternal life abiding in him.*"

The saloon men and barkeepers do not have it. Infidels and agnostics do not have it. The cultured scholastic agnostic knows nothing of it.

Here is a significant fact: If the men and women who are spending their time and money in philanthropic efforts to help the less-favored knew what eternal life did for men, it would change their whole outlook on philanthropy.

When criminals and the lawless receive eternal life, they become law-abiding citizens and worthy examples in society. Thieves become honest; drunkards become sober. No case is incurable.

It destroys the cause of friction in homes and every department of life. In all walks of life, it eliminates selfishness, and in its place gives a new kind of love and a new outlook on life.

WHAT IT DOES

The new kind of life recreates man. It actually makes him a new creation. Paul expresses it this way: "*Therefore, if anyone is in Christ, he is a new creation* [or new species]; *old things have passed away; behold, all things have become new*" (2 Corinthians 5:17).

The worst criminals become evangelists and preachers.

The most godless of men become faithful husbands and fathers.

The gambler and the outcast become clean, worthy citizens.

MORE FACTS

Children born of parents who have received this new life and have walked in the light of it are never found among criminals.

Take this as an illustration: Here is a father and mother who have never received eternal life. They have two children. Then they receive eternal life. Several children are born to them.

As the children grow up, you can see a vast difference in them. The first two lack some element of fineness of spirit. They are hard to discipline. They have no religious inclinations.

The other children respond to religious training. They are eagerly seek the things that go with eternal life. They are different. There is refinement and culture in their spirits that the others do not have, though they are born of the same parents.

The first two children sow their wild oats; they are hard to discipline.

The children born after the parents received eternal life never sow wild oats and are easier to discipline. They have finer intellects.

Another remarkable feature: Boys and girls in their teens who receive eternal life and have an opportunity to let that life dominate their lives are 10 to 50 percent more mentally efficient than they were before. Something comes into them that affects their mental processes and governs their morals.

You cannot find one boy or girl who has eternal life in a house of correction for juveniles.

Hardly a boy or girl are juvenile criminals whose parents had eternal life and walked in the light of it before the children were born and while they were growing.

I have said enough, if it is true, to change the attitude of social workers toward the criminal world.

Crime is increasing. The youth of our nation are hard to restrain. Parental discipline is almost ignored. Why? Because something has been lost out of our theological institutions, pulpits, and schools. It is the knowledge of eternal life.

WHAT IS ETERNAL LIFE?

Eternal life is the nature of God. Jesus said, *"I have come that they may have life [zoe], and that they may have it more abundantly"* (John 10:10).

John 1:4 says, *"In Him was life, and the life was the light of men."*

That seems strange. Read it over again.

Notice that the life that was in Christ has become the light of civilization, has caused the mental development and the creative ability in man.

No heathen country has ever needed a patent law or a copyright law until eternal life was brought to them. The creative genius of mankind sprang into being in the second generation after they had received eternal life.

Eternal life is the creative nature of God, and we have come to recognize the fact that man is a spirit created in the image and likeness of God and can receive God's creative nature.

Man was created to be the eternal companion of God.

Quoting from Psalm 8:4, an eminent Hebrew scholar asked, *"What is man that You are mindful of him?"* He noted that God made man "but a shadow, a shade, lower than God" and yet "*crowned him with glory and honor*" (verse 5).

That was the original man, the first man. He was made as nearly like God as God could create a being.

Man is an eternal being. Now you can understand that he is in God's class. He was created so that he could receive the nature of God and become God's actual child.

Now you can see the genius of God! God wanted a companion. He wanted children. But He wanted to glorify man, so He gave him the privilege of being the parent of his children.

God planned originally that man should become a partaker of His divine nature.

When man committed that unthinkable crime of high treason in the garden, he forfeited his right to the nature of God and became the partaker of the nature of God's enemy. That nature is called spiritual death, as opposed to God's nature, which is spiritual life.

One produces crime, misery, murder, mortality, and death. The other gives life, love, and light—unselfishness. These are the sweet fruits of the recreated spirit. One makes earth a hell, while the other produces heaven on earth.

Now we can understand, "*In Him was life*" (John 1:4)—and that life is the light, the development of man. That life has given to us the best that is in our civilization. It has given to us all our mechanical and chemical discoveries and inventions.

MAN IS A SPIRIT

For a long time, we were puzzled about the creative element in man.

We saw early on that it would not come from the reasoning faculties because they receive all their impulses and knowledge from the five senses.

Where was the ability that produced poetry? It came flooding our minds with beautiful rhythm and couplets of words that we had never used before.

From where did the music come that thrilled us—the harmonies, melodies, symphonies, orchestrations? Where did they come from? They weren't reasoned out. They simply came floating into our consciousness from a source we did not know. It was something with which our imaginations were unacquainted.

It came forth as something new in the form of intricate machinery.

This didn't come by experimentation, as we have achieved it, in chemistry.

Where did those pictures of marvelous art come from that we see in drawings and paintings? They came from the human spirit.

Eternal life is given to man's spirit, the part of him that is recreated or born again, and this human spirit is the creative element in man.

When the spirit receives eternal life, it begins a war against the senses that rule the mind, which has received all of its impulses from the human body. It demands ascendancy over the mind. This takes place as the mind is renewed and comes into harmony and fellowship with a recreated spirit.

All creative ability is in the human spirit. Sense knowledge has never produced an inventor. Sense knowledge can only experiment and follow the blueprints of the recreated human spirit.

Now we understand why there are no inventors in heathen lands. Man must first receive the creative nature of God.

2

THE GREATEST BIOLOGICAL FACT IN HUMAN EXPERIENCE

God is the designer and creator of the universe.

Men who have studied botany, biology, and metallurgy have been amazed at the ability of the Creator. The creative, inventive genius of God staggers the human reason.

It would not be strange then if man, who is in God's class, could receive this creative energy in the new birth.

Some of us have come to recognize that the human spirit is the fountain out of which all the creative energy flows. We recognize the fact that pure human reason or sense knowledge has never produced an inventor, a great poet, or a creator in any department of human culture.

This fact gave me a mental shock when I first saw it. Then the question came, "What is there about this eternal life that caused men to become inventors, scientists, chemists, and biologists?"

Natural human reason or sense knowledge had made philosophers of men. But what is philosophy? It is a vain search for reality.

No philosopher ever found it. The philosopher cannot find anything outside of himself unless it comes from some other being.

Aristotle and other philosophers of Greece did not give to the world a civilization. They did not give to the world a great educational system nor an age of electricity or mechanics. They didn't discover. They never created. The fact is, they did not give us anything except mental concepts and theories.

It is a remarkable thing that when a man receives eternal life and allows it to develop in him, his creative energy is at once awakened. It changes his mental processes. It quickens his sense of perception.

All the knowledge that we have in our colleges, universities, and technical schools has come to us through the five senses—seeing, hearing, tasting, smelling, and feeling. Man has no means of gaining knowledge except through these five channels.

The limitations of sense knowledge are apparent to every thinking man. He cannot know beyond the contacts that he makes with these five senses.

Sense knowledge men have never made creators, inventors, or chemists. They cannot find God. They cannot find the human spirit. They cannot find the reason for man, or the source of life or motion.

Sense knowledge carries them to the frontier of human investigation but can take them no further.

Then revelation knowledge comes to their rescue. God imparts to the man of the five senses His own nature. This recreates his human spirit and reacts upon his thinking processes.

In our investigation, we have proven that when young people receive eternal life, it increases their mental efficiency from 10 to 50 percent, and in many cases, more than 100 percent.

If the new convert is properly instructed in the Word—taught to act upon it, taught to depend upon the God inside of him, taught his privileges and rights in prayer, and taught his rights as a son in the Father's family—his mental efficiency increases amazingly.

We have discovered that the human spirit is the source of all creative energy, that it does not come from the reasoning faculties. It directs them.

No nation has ever needed a patent law or a copyright law until it received eternal life. They can follow blueprints, they can imitate, and they can take one of our machines apart and build from it, but they cannot create a machine.

Natural man can only learn by experimentation. Sense knowledge has no other means of learning except by imitation or experimentation. It is said that Edison experimented over 3,000 times before he developed our electric light.

The natural human spirit is not creative, but when this creative nature of God comes into it, it at once has creative possibilities. All it needs is to be developed.

This is not a theory. This is an absolute fact. It is the most revolutionary fact connected with biology.

SOME BIOLOGICAL MIRACLES

I used to wonder what it was that made some who had been criminals such enthusiastic Christians. I knew that there was nothing in the forgiveness of sin that would do it. I knew that if all God did for a man was to forget his past and pardon it, the man would go on and have another past.

Forgiveness has no power to change a man's nature.

Then I found out about eternal life.

You may take the worst crook who ever walked in the underworld of our great cities, let him receive eternal life, and he will become at once an honorable, trustworthy person.

Religion will not do it, but eternal life does.

Take the habitual criminal. The moment he receives eternal life, his days of crime are over.

Go through our penal institutions. You cannot find a habitual criminal who has eternal life. If they have received eternal life, they are no longer criminals.

There are no habitual drinkers who have eternal life. Eternal life absolutely changes their nature.

The chronic *hobo* who lives in the jungles of our big cities becomes an honest laborer when he receives eternal life.

No boys or girls who receive eternal life ever become criminals.

Here is the greatest biological fact that has ever confronted the scientific mind.

If what we have just said is true, and it is true, we have discovered the secret of changing the morals of men and women. By morals, we mean conduct.

Scientists have been searching to find some method whereby they could change criminals into honest men. This is the secret.

SOLVES LABOR PROBLEMS

It is also the solution to the labor and capital problem. The capitalist who has received eternal life and walks in the Word can never take advantage of his employee. It would end the labor strikes and strife.

Wouldn't it be a good idea to have an intelligent understanding of this problem?

We are spending millions to solve the problem of labor and capital.

We have built up an army of labor racketeers. Many of them, according to reports, come from the underworld. They saw an opportunity to victimize the laboring man and extort money from the manufacturer at the same time.

All this would stop being.

This is not a theory—not philosophy, metaphysics, or psychology. This is real Christianity, the thing that Jesus brought to the world.

We have in our factories, our great industries, and multitudes of people who can follow blueprints, but we have only a few who have creative ability.

You will find in the majority of cases that those with creative ability have received eternal life or else have parents or grandparents who had it.

ITS EFFECTS ON CHILDREN

The children of parents who have received eternal life are mentally superior to those of parents who have not received eternal life. They are more easily influenced to accept Christianity than are those who have come out of irreligious homes. You can very seldom find a criminal whose parents had received eternal life before he was born.

Following World War I, the United States government made a thorough investigation of the leaders of our great business organizations like the Sugar Trust and the Steel Trust. They discovered that 30 percent of these great leaders were the sons of clergymen and that 25 percent of them were the sons of lawyers, doctors, bankers, and college professors.

Do you see the reaction of eternal life upon the descendants of those who have received it?

We have one family in the United States that has produced hundreds of criminals. We have other families such as the Adams family, the Scudder family, and the Edwards family that have turned out hundreds of leaders of society and almost no criminals.

Why? Because they were the children of men and women who had received the life and nature of God, who were new creations.

WHAT IT MEANS TO THE INDIVIDUAL

The new creation is the most outstanding miracle of human experience. To think that a man can receive into his spirit the very nature and life of God is an incredible thing to the natural mind.

> *But the natural man does not receive the things of the Spirit of God, for they are foolishness to him; nor can he know them, because they are spiritually discerned.* (1 Corinthians 2:14)

The natural man cannot understand the things of the Spirit of God. His mind receives all its impulses and knowledge from the five senses—seeing, hearing, smelling, tasting, and feeling.

There is no other means for the natural man to obtain knowledge. His spirit is not responsive to divine things. God cannot reveal things to him; he cannot understand spiritual things. Consequently, the only knowledge the natural man can receive is that which has come through his or someone else's five senses.

All the knowledge we teach in our colleges, universities, and technical schools comes from the five senses.

We are making a distinction between sense knowledge and revelation knowledge, between the natural or physical man and the spiritual man.

I do not condemn the natural man because he doubts miracles or because he doubts the Bible. It would be a perfectly normal thing for him to do this because he cannot understand either. They are in a realm above him. Natural man is spiritually dead.

And you He made alive, who were dead in trespasses and sins, in which you once walked according to the course of this world, according to the prince of the power of the air, the spirit who now works in the sons of disobedience, among whom also we all once conducted ourselves in the lusts of our flesh, fulfilling the desires of the flesh and of the mind, and were by nature children of wrath. (Ephesians 2:1–3)

Death here means union with Satan, a partaker of the satanic nature.

I know that some of you who read this will be shocked by it. I was at first and thought I could never tell it to anyone. It is like cancer, tuberculosis, or any other deadly disease. It is not nice to talk about, but it must be faced.

Spiritual death has to be faced. That is the reason Jesus came: to give man, who was spiritually dead, a new nature.

God is love. When God imparts His nature to us, we have a love nature.

THE EFFECT ON THE HOME

Do you see what this would mean in a home?

In a home where the husband and wife have lived very unhappily, have quarreled and had their continual differences, there is a great need for this new kind of life.

It is more than likely that they would have separated had it not been for the children.

Now they have both received eternal life. They have discovered the new way of life. They no longer quarrel. The things that caused their differences before have ceased to be or are passed over without friction. They have new natures.

THE EFFECT ON THE CHILDREN

The effect on the children is tremendous.

One little boy said, "Papa, what has happened to you and Mama? You don't fight anymore. You haven't sworn at me for a long time. What is it, Daddy?"

The father took him in his arms and said, "Son, I have received eternal life. I am a Jesus man now."

That new life changes everything. Children who grow up in this atmosphere seldom go wrong. They are guarded from it by something within them.

It is deeply important that every man and woman who is thinking of marriage and a family should consider this question: Have I a right to bring children into the world until I myself have received eternal life?

This is a problem for the prospective father and mother to solve.

You will have a higher type of children. They will be more easily governed. They will be more trustworthy. Even if they do not become Christians, they will always bear the mark of their parents' union with Christ.

It means a happier home. But it also means something else. It means that your life comes into fellowship with the Father's life. It means that you have God as your Father and that you are His child. It means that you have God's ability to assist you in life's fight.

3

THE NEED OF ETERNAL LIFE

The subject of eternal life can well be called another lost truth. The church has never majored eternal life, and yet it was the reason for Christ's coming. John 10:10 says, *"I have come that they may have life, and that they may have it more abundantly."*

The word *life* used here is from the Greek word *zoe*. It is the word used in connection with eternal life. The other word, *psuche*, means natural life and all other forms of life.

Man is spiritually dead.

And you He made alive, who were dead in trespasses and sins. (Ephesians 2:1)

Spiritual death is the nature of the adversary. When Adam sinned in the garden, he became a partaker of satanic nature. This nature has been the cause of all the sin, misery, and sickness of the human race. It has given to man an inferiority complex, a sense of unworthiness, and a sense of sin. It has given him hatred, jealousy, and bitterness.

All the crimes and miseries of the ages are the result of this nature that man possesses. The reason that man cannot stand right with God is that his nature is enmity against God.

Romans 8:7 (RSV) tells us, *"For the mind that is set on the flesh is hostile to God; it does not submit to God's law, indeed it cannot."*

This nature must be taken out of man, and a new nature must be given to him.

Our popular Christianity is the product in part of the Dark Ages. It is not the Christianity of the Pauline Epistles. Consequently, there is much said about sin and repentance for sin, but there is little said about eternal life.

If it were possible for God to simply forgive a sinner his sins, it would do him no good because he would go on sinning. The sinner must have a new nature. He must be recreated. This recreation can only be accomplished by imparting to him a new nature.

Through Jesus, we become *"partakers of the divine nature, having escaped the corruption that is in the world through lust"* (2 Peter 1:4).

That corruption is spiritual death. We only escape it by the new birth, receiving this new nature.

> *For God so loved the world that He gave His only begotten Son, that whoever believes in Him should not perish but have everlasting life.* (John 3:16)

> *Jesus did many other signs in the presence of His disciples, which are not written in this book; but these are written that you may believe that Jesus is the Christ, the Son of God, and that believing you may have life in His name.*
> (John 20:30–31)

> *In Him was life, and the life was the light of men.* (John 1:4)

Jesus came to bring to man a new nature, eternal life. Until man has this new nature, he is living in the realm of spiritual death, and he is a subject of Satan.

> At that time you were without Christ, being aliens from the commonwealth of Israel and strangers from the covenants of promise, having no hope and without God in the world.
> (Ephesians 2:12)

Without this new nature, man is alienated from the life of God. He cannot come into God's presence. He cannot fellowship with God. His nature is enmity against God. His only hope lies in a new creation.

In John 5:24, Jesus said, *"Most assuredly, I say to you, he who hears My word and believes in Him who sent Me has everlasting life, and shall not come into judgment, but has passed from death into life."*

The one who receives eternal life passes out of the realm of death, Satan's dominion and realm, into the realm of life.

There is no judgment for the man who has passed out of Satan's realm into God's realm. He passes out of death into life. It is an actual birth out of Satan's family into God's family.

It is mentioned in Colossians 1:13: *"He has delivered us from the power of darkness and conveyed us into the kingdom of the Son of His love."*

That is the new birth.

> Therefore, if anyone is in Christ, he is a new creation; old things have passed away; behold, all things have become new. Now all things are of God, who has reconciled us to Himself through Jesus Christ, and has given us the ministry of reconciliation.
> (2 Corinthians 5:17–18)

This is an actual transition of man from Satan's family into God's family.

When he accepts Christ as Savior and confesses Him as Lord, God breathes eternal life into him. That drives out the satanic nature and makes him a new creation. With the new creation comes a new mode of life.

> We know that we have passed from death to life, because we love the brethren. He who does not love his brother abides in death. Whoever hates his brother is a murderer, and you know that no murderer has eternal life abiding in him.
>
> (1 John 3:14–15)

The new life that has come into us is God's life. *"God is love"* (1 John 4:8), so it is a new love that has come into our life.

He who does not love *"abides in death."* He has never yet been born again.

Christianity is not a religion. It is not joining a church. It is not having your sins forgiven. It is receiving the nature of God, eternal life. Until one does receive eternal life, he is not a child of God.

We are children, not by adoption only, but by an actual birth of our spirits. When you accept Christ as Savior and confess Him as your Lord, God gives you eternal life, His own nature. That eternal life is imparted to your spirit.

Your spirit is made a new creation. The spirit begins to react upon the mind; and the mind as it meditates and practices the Word becomes renewed. The mind is recreated. It gets a new sense of God, a new vision, and it can understand the Word now and enjoy it.

Previously, the Word was dark, mysterious, and uninteresting. Now it is a living thing.

> *The words that I speak to you are spirit, and they are life.*
>
> (John 6:63)

> *Truly, truly, I say to you, he who believes has eternal life.*
>
> (John 6:47 RSV)

You can see the distinction here between mental assent, which says, "Yes, I know that eternal life belongs to man," and real faith that says, "I know that I have eternal life."

When we believe, or act on the Word, we become possessors of eternal life. We pass out of Satan's dominion into the family of God.

And this is the testimony: that God has given us eternal life, and this life is in His Son. He who has the Son has life; he who does not have the Son of God does not have life. These things I have written to you who believe in the name of the Son of God, that you may know that you have eternal life.
(1 John 5:11–13)

The philosophical and metaphysical religions have no eternal life. They simply revamp the natural with some new theory of life.

The men and women who accept these religions have never been born again. They are spiritually dead, though they may have become very religious.

The natural man can become very religious. His spirit nature hungers after God, and it reaches out after anything that seems to help and bring him into a better spiritual condition. However, he cannot find or know God until he receives God's nature, until He becomes a child of God by an actual birth.

Receiving eternal life is very simple. We know according to the prophet Isaiah that God laid our iniquities upon Jesus.

All we like sheep have gone astray; we have turned, every one, to his own way; and the Lord has laid on Him the iniquity of us all. (Isaiah 53:6)

Jesus was God's substitute for the human race. We know that Jesus bore our sins and diseases in His body on the tree. We know that *"He has appeared to put away sin by the sacrifice of Himself"* (Hebrews 9:26).

We know that by that one sacrifice of Himself, He satisfied the claims of justice, put sin away, and made it possible for man to become a new creation, the righteousness of God in Christ.

> But as many as received Him, to them He gave the right to become children of God, to those who believe in His name.
>
> (John 1:12)

Romans 10:9–11 tells us that if we take Jesus Christ as Savior, confess Him as Lord, and believe that God raised Him from the dead, God immediately takes us to be His children and gives us eternal life. *"For with the heart one believes unto righteousness, and with the mouth confession is made unto salvation"* (verse 10).

You make this your confession: "I have taken Him as my Savior. I have confessed Him as my Lord. God has taken me to be His child and has given me His righteousness and eternal life."

This perfectly harmonizes with 2 Corinthians 5:21: *"He made Him who knew no sin to be sin for us, that we might become the righteousness of God in Him."*

Eternal life makes man righteous. Eternal life makes man a lover. Eternal life makes man a Father-pleaser.

Eternal life is the most important thing in life today.

It is not a question of whether one is a church member, or whether one has been confirmed or baptized. The real question is, "Have you received eternal life?" If you have, you are God's child. If you have not, you may be a minister, you may be a bishop or a pope, but you are still spiritually dead, without God and without hope.

One needs to meditate on the Scriptures until the new creation fact becomes a living reality. When you know you are a new creation, you know that Satan has no dominion over you. You know that Colossians 1:13–14 is absolutely true:

> *He has delivered us from the power of darkness and conveyed us into the kingdom of the Son of His love, in whom we have redemption through His blood, the forgiveness of sins.*

The new birth is an actual transition out of Satan's authority and dominion. Satan has no legal right to reign over the new creation.

Romans 6:14 is not only a classic truth, but a tremendous truth: *"For sin shall not have dominion over you, for you are not under law but under grace."*

Another translation (WNT) says: *"For Sin shall not be lord over you."*

Sin's power over you is Satan's power. Satan has been dethroned. He belongs to the dethroned powers. Your redemption means the breaking of Satan's dominion.

Ephesians 1:7 tells us, *"In Him [Jesus] we have redemption through His blood, the forgiveness of sins, according to the riches of His grace."*

Your redemption made possible the new creation. The new creation is under the lordship of Jesus. *"He is the head of the body, the church, who is the beginning, the firstborn from the dead"* (Colossians 1:18).

He is the Lord of the new creation. He is the supplier of every need. He is the protector. He is the Good Shepherd and our Lord.

You need to meditate on this truth until it burns in your very being, so that when sickness lays hold upon your body, you say with certainty, "Disease cannot touch the temple of the Holy Spirit. My body is the temple of God. God dwells in this new creation. He is my Father. I am His child. Disease cannot reign over His body. I am not my own. This body belongs to my Lord. I am but a custodian of it. As a custodian, I refuse to have disease in my body to dishonor the indwelling presence of my Lord."

We must become new creation conscious. Previously, we were sin conscious and failure conscious. Now we become God conscious and Son conscious.

We know that we have the strength of God in us, the life of God. The very substance and being of God has become a part of our spirits. We know that we have a right to associate and fellowship with the Father on terms of utter equality because Jesus is our righteousness, and we, by this new creation, have become the righteousness of God in Him.

The new creation should never be under condemnation. If sin comes, we should confess it, put it away, and walk on with Him.

The new creation has an Advocate, Jesus Christ, the righteous.

If we confess our sins, He is faithful and just to forgive us our sins and to cleanse us from all unrighteousness. (1 John 1:9)

This leaves us in the Father's presence as clean and as pure as though we had not sinned.

The new creation is not a servant. The new creation is a son or daughter, a child of the Father.

Therefore you are no longer a slave but a son, and if a son, then an heir of God through Christ. (Galatians 4:7)

The new creation takes a son's place in the Father's heart and lives as a son of God among men. He is now an ambassador on the behalf of Christ. He is a representative of the new race of men.

First John 5:13 becomes a reality in the heart: "*These things I have written to you who believe in the name of the Son of God, that you may know that you have eternal life.*"

You have the very nature and life of God in you. The knowledge of this fact gives one a quietness, a sense of oneness with God. You are one with Him just as that bay is one with the ocean because the tides flow into the bay.

God's nature flows into you. You are linked with God. God and you are identified.

Healing, strength, success, and victory are all a part of this new creation life that has been made a reality by God's imparting His nature to us.

4

MANNER OF LIFE

The church has made more of the manner of living than it has of the life that would make our living like the Master's. Our teachers have never majored the Greek word *zoe*, which is translated "eternal life." They have never realized its place and significance in the plan of redemption.

Jesus majored it. It means the life, the nature of God. To bring this life to the world was the reason that Jesus came.

In John 10:10, Jesus says, *"I have come that they may have life, and that they may have it more abundantly."*

Men needed eternal life because they were spiritually dead. This eternal life is the nature of God. Man's need was for God's nature.

If we go back to Genesis, we remember that God placed two trees in the garden of Eden. One was the Tree of Life. It would have united man with God. He had the opportunity, but he did not partake of it.

Then Jesus came bringing the thing that Adam ignored in the garden. *"For God so loved the world that He gave His only begotten*

Son, that whoever believes in Him should not perish but have everlasting life" (John 3:16).

John 5:24 tells us that when we believe, we pass out of death into life. That means that we pass out of the realm of spiritual death into the realm of eternal life.

Perhaps the most outstanding Scripture is John 20:30–31:

> Jesus did many other signs in the presence of His disciples, which are not written in this book; but these are written that you may believe that Jesus is the Christ, the Son of God, and that believing you may have life in His name.

Many call these verses "the little gospel." The reason for redemption, for all that God did in Christ, was to give to man eternal life. "*Truly, truly, I say to you, he who believes has eternal life*" (John 6:47 RSV).

We receive eternal life by accepting Jesus Christ as our Savior. Another word that is used, which means "manner of life," "conduct," or "conversation," is *anastrophee*.

Ephesians 4:22 (RSV) says, "*Put off your old nature which belongs to your former manner of life and is corrupt through deceitful lusts.*"

We have majored conduct, conversation, and habits because they are in the sense realm. They have always appealed to the babes in Christ. We like to be told what we can do and what we cannot do.

Another Greek word, *bios*, sometimes translated "manner of life," is used eleven times, mostly in Paul's epistles. It is from this word that we get our word *biology*. *Bios* is not used interchangeably with *zoe*, which is eternal life.

The Gospel of John opens with this Greek word, *zoe*. John 1:4 says, "*In Him was life, and the life was the light of men.*"

Man receives the very nature and life of God, which puts him into God's class of being. This is something greater than the forgiveness of sins, baptism, joining the church, or confirmation. It is receiving God's life into our spirits. It is receiving the creative ability of God.

This is significant. We can see now the imperative need for receiving eternal life. It is a crime that the church has never majored in this.

Notice that passing out of death into life means being translated out of the kingdom of Satan *"into the kingdom of the Son of His love"* (Colossians 1:13). It is becoming *"partakers of the divine nature"* (2 Peter 1:4).

> *For as the Father has life in Himself, so He has granted the Son to have life in Himself.* (John 5:26)

In other words, God is the fountain of this life, and Jesus brought it to the human race. It is a remarkable thing, when we think of it, that God is the fountain of eternal life, and Jesus came to bring this life to man. We will study this more fully in another chapter.

5

RECREATION OF THE HUMAN SPIRIT

Our theological thinkers have never majored in this phase of teaching. It is the crux of the whole Pauline revelation, the ultimate toward which all of God's plans move. Man, sin-ruled and Satan-dominated, held in bondage by the unseen forces of spiritual darkness, is to be recreated, made a new creation, taken out of the family of Satan, and translated *"into the kingdom of the Son of His love"* (Colossians 1:13) on legal grounds.

This is the solution of the human problem: God giving His nature and His love to fallen man.

He is no longer a fallen man. He is a new creation man united with Jesus Christ, the head of the new creation. He is the "raised together with Christ" man.

> *Therefore, if anyone is in Christ, he is a new creation; old things have passed away; behold, all things have become new.*
> (2 Corinthians 5:17)

His old sin consciousness, his old fallen life, his old sin life, and his old evil habits that grew out of spiritual death have passed away. He is a new creation, a new being.

The Father has no memory of his past life. He is a newborn babe. His old past life has stopped being in the mind of justice and in the mind of the Father. A new creation has come into being through grace.

Second Corinthians 5:18 says, *"Now all things are of God, who has reconciled us to Himself through Jesus Christ, and has given us the ministry of reconciliation."* This is not the ministry of condemnation that we have had for the last hundred years, but a ministry of reconciliation.

We have reckoned unto men their trespasses. We have kept them *trespass minded*. We have kept them conscious of their weaknesses and failings. We have preached sin instead of eternal life. We have preached judgment instead of reconciliation, when God has committed unto us His Word of reconciliation.

We have that Word. We have that message. It is ours to give to the world. We have become new creations. We have been recreated by love.

Love has been imparted to our spirit beings. *"God is love"* (1 John 4:8), and God's nature is love, but God is also life as the Author of life. So He has imparted to us His life nature, His love nature.

God has imparted His nature to us, making us new creations. That nature is righteousness. It is holiness. It is reality. It is love. It has been imparted to us. We are ambassadors on behalf of Christ, and we are entreating the world to be reconciled to God.

Why? Because Him who knew no sin God made to become sin that *"we might become the righteousness of God in Him"* (2 Corinthians 5:21). God made Jesus sin so He could make us righteous through the new creation. We have become new creations and *"the righteousness of God in Him."*

We have a reconciling message of love to give to the world. It is not a message of condemnation but of reconciliation, not of judgment but of love.

Jesus was made sin, was judged, and suffered all that we would have suffered had we rejected Him. By our acceptance of Him, we enter into all that He purchased for us. This message is not an appeal to human reason or sense knowledge. It is the Father's appeal to our spirits.

We ought to understand that the Father does not reveal Himself to our reasoning faculties but to our spirits. Our reasoning faculties can only comprehend the things that the five senses convey to them. Outside of that, the reasoning faculties are dumb and unfruitful.

When our spirits are recreated, they receive eternal life. We can know the Father. We can enjoy fellowship with Him through His Word. We become so utterly identified with Him, so utterly one with Him, that Jesus as the vine with us as the branches is the only suitable illustration of this new and beautiful relationship. (See John 15:5.)

We are a part of the vine life. We are bearing the love fruit of the vine life. Our spirits enjoy the reality of Christ in the Word.

Our minds may not be able to grasp it; but if we let our minds be renewed by acting on the Word and meditating on it, our minds and spirits will come into sweet fellowship with each other.

The recreated human spirit never grows old. It has received eternal life. It has become one with the Father.

Our bodies will grow old. Our minds will grow old because they derive all their knowledge from the body. If our spirits can gain the ascendancy over our bodies, they will keep our minds from aging, and our bodies in a vigorous, healthy, youthful condition.

Sense knowledge wanes with the senility of the senses. The senses will wear out and lose their freshness and beauty unless they are renewed by a recreated spirit.

The development of our recreated spirits comes by meditating on the Word, acting on the Word, and letting the Word live in us and become a part of us.

SOME FACTS

Christianity is a relationship between the Father and His family. It is not a religion. It is not having your sins forgiven. It is not joining the church.

It is being made a new creation in Christ. It is being born again, born from above. It is receiving the nature and life of God. It is being united with Christ.

For if we have been united together in the likeness of His death, certainly we also shall be in the likeness of His resurrection. (Romans 6:5)

We are united with Him in resurrection life.

The new creation is to enjoy the dominion that Adam lost in the fall.

God speaks out His heart's dream here:

I will give you a new heart and put a new spirit within you; I will take the heart of stone out of your flesh and give you a heart of flesh. I will put My Spirit within you and cause you to walk in My statutes, and you will keep My judgments and do them. (Ezekiel 36:26–27)

Man was to have a new heart. That means his heart was to be recreated.

When the Lord speaks of the heart, He means the spirit, the real man.

The new creation is the outstanding miracle of redemption. On the day of Pentecost, when the Spirit recreated one hundred and twenty in the upper room, God began the *new thing*. They had more than forgiveness of sin. They had new natures. It was the union of love with man.

God is love. God's nature becomes man's nature. Man becomes a lover. It is a new order of things.

Second Corinthians 5:17 says, *"Therefore, if anyone is in Christ, he is a new creation."* They are a new species, new lovers. The expression *"new creation"* means a new thing, something unheard of before.

This new man was an unknown thing just as the first Adam was an unknown being. This new love nature means that the old order of selfishness is ended, and the new love life has begun.

The new creation is a God-man born of heaven. He is like the sample, Jesus. He is God's superman. He is to walk in the realm of the supernatural. He is to be ruled by the Lord. He has been ruled by Satan.

He is called in the righteous one, the God-made one. *"My righteous one shall live by faith"* (Hebrews 10:38 RSV).

He is the new love man ruled by our love Lord, Jesus. By nature, he was a child of wrath. By the new nature, he is a child of God. The God who created man in the beginning is recreating man now.

The recreated man is born from above:

Jesus answered and said to him, "Most assuredly, I say to you, unless one is born again, he cannot see the kingdom of God." Nicodemus said to Him, "How can a man be born when he is old? Can he enter a second time into his mother's womb and be born?" Jesus answered, "Most assuredly, I say to you, unless one is born of water and the Spirit, he cannot enter the kingdom of God. That which is born of the flesh is flesh, and that which is born of the Spirit is spirit. Do not marvel that I said to you, 'You must be born again.' The wind blows where it wishes, and you hear the sound of it, but cannot tell where it comes from and where it goes. So is everyone who is born of the Spirit." (John 3:3–8)

The born-again man is born of the Word and of the Spirit. Read these verses carefully and you will notice that he is recreated by the will of the Father. He is a wanted child.

James 1:18 says, "*Of His own will He brought us forth by the word of truth.*"

We are recreated by the Spirit through the Word.

Having been born again, not of corruptible seed but incorruptible, through the word of God which lives and abides forever.
(1 Peter 1:23)

No man recreates himself. It is purely the work of God. The only part we have in it is to consent to God's giving us His nature and to recognize the lordship of the new head of the new creation, Jesus.

For by grace you have been saved through faith, and that not of yourselves; it is the gift of God, not of works, lest anyone should boast. For we are His workmanship, created in Christ Jesus for good works, which God prepared beforehand that we should walk in them. (Ephesians 2:8–10)

When you know that you have been recreated by God Himself, you know that the work is satisfactory to the Author of the work. It gives you a real foundation for faith.

Our chief difficulty has been the sense of unworthiness that has robbed us of faith and fellowship with the Father. This is due to our ignorance of what we are in Christ and what the new birth means to the Father and may mean to us.

Ephesians 4:24 encourages us to *"put on the new man which was created according to God, in true righteousness and holiness."* Another translation (WNT) says, *"That new and better self which has been created to resemble God in the righteousness and holiness which come from the truth."*

We are created in righteousness. We are created out of the very nature and heart of the Father, so that when He declares that we are created of righteousness, holiness, and reality or truth, we know that we can stand before the Father without any sense of guilt or sin.

We know that this new creation is the righteousness of God in Christ.

> *These things I have written to you who believe in the name of the Son of God, that you may know that you have eternal life.* (1 John 5:13)

So then, eternal life is received in Jesus's name.

The climax of redemption is outlined in this epistle:

> *For as many as are led by the Spirit of God, these are sons of God. For you did not receive the spirit of bondage again to fear, but you received the Spirit of adoption by whom we cry out, "Abba, Father." The Spirit Himself bears witness with our spirit that we are children of God, and if children, then heirs—heirs of God and joint heirs with Christ, if indeed we suffer with Him, that we may also be glorified together.*
> (Romans 8:14–17)

This is the objective toward which God was working: to bring man into the actual relationship of a son through his partaking of God's nature, eternal life.

Galatians 4:5–7 says, *"To redeem those who were under the law, that we* [the Jewish people] *might receive the adoption as sons. And because you are sons, God has sent forth the Spirit of His Son into your hearts, crying out, 'Abba, Father!' Therefore you are no longer a slave but a son, and if a son, then an heir of God through Christ."*

The Jews were the servants of God; we are the children of God.

Beloved, now we are children of God. (1 John 3:2)

He made Him who knew no sin to be sin for us, that we might become the righteousness of God in Him.
(2 Corinthians 5:21)

Who were born, not of blood, nor of the will of the flesh, nor of the will of man, but of God. (John 1:13)

This should forever settle the question of whether there is anything that an unsaved man can do to give to himself the new birth outside of his acceptance of Christ as Savior and Lord. All of his crying, weeping, repenting, and confessing of sins has no bearing upon it whatsoever. This is hard for us to accept because we have been ruled by the teaching of the Dark Ages, the teaching of works.

The church is under bondage today to the blend of Hinduism, Grecian philosophy, and the Christianity that we find during the Middle Ages.

All that Luther saw was justification by faith. He had no clear conception of a new birth, righteousness, God as a Father, or our place as sons and daughters of God. He saw it vaguely. He saw one truth. That one truth brought him out of bondage and gave to Germany a new civilization.

First John 5:1 says, "*Whoever believes that Jesus is the Christ is born of God.*" Then a little later, we read, "*For whatever is born of God overcomes the world. And this is the victory that has overcome the world—our faith*" (verse 4).

The new creation is an overcomer. He is begotten of God. He is united with God. He is a partaker of God's nature.

6

SPIRITUAL DEATH

The spiritual swampland of the human race, the soil out of which all sin has sprung, came into man in the garden of Eden when man disobeyed God and made partnership with Satan. Satan imparted to him his own substance and nature so that this thing called death passed into him. It has followed down the stream of human life through the ages. Every man has been touched by it.

Spiritual death gave satanic dominion to us. It separated us from God. It made of us criminals and renegades from the will of God. Spiritual death gave to us mortality with all its diseases and pains that end in the physical dissolution of the human body.

Spiritual death is the parent of all sorrow, grief, and tears. It marred not only the human world but the animal and vegetable world as well. It is the curse that came upon everything at the fall of man.

Man is not lost because of what he does but because of what he is.

You can see now that forgiveness of what a man does would not reach the issue. He must have a new nature.

This old nature must be taken away, and a new one must fill its place.

That is why Jesus said, *"I have come that they may have life, and that they may have it more abundantly"* (John 10:10). That life is the nature of God.

The spiritually dead man is to receive this new nature, eternal life, which will make him a new creation in Christ Jesus.

7

WHAT ETERNAL LIFE DOES

No matter from what angle you look at eternal life as it contacts man's spirit, it is miraculous.

Eternal life is the nature of God the Father. When we become *"partakers of the divine nature"* (2 Peter 1:4), we become united with the Father.

Jesus illustrated this in John 15:5, saying, *"I am the vine, you are the branches."* The vine's life is divine life. The life in the branches is a part of the life of the vine. So we become united with God. This is the phenomena of Christianity.

What could it do for the people if everyone in the nation were partakers of the divine nature. How godlike it would be!

If every member of a family were partakers of the divine nature, what a family it would be! That would solve every economic problem and every social issue that confronts us as a people.

Every home would be a safe place for a baby to be born and reared. It would never hear cursing or witness drunkenness. It would solve the home problem. There would be no divorces. When a man and woman receive eternal life and let that life dominate them, each one lives for the other's happiness.

The most amazing fact is that the old selfish Adamic nature is eliminated, and God's nature takes its place.

Beloved, let us love one another, for love is of God; and everyone who loves is born of God and knows God. He who does not love does not know God, for God is love. (1 John 4:7–8)

Here we see the evidence of the new birth: that we love one another. If one does not love, he is not born again. This is God's criteria.

There should never be the question of whether this person or that person is a child of God. If he walks in love, he is a child of God. If he does not walk in love, he is either out of fellowship and not walking with the Father, or else he has never received eternal life.

Romans 15:1 (RSV) says, *"We who are strong ought to bear with the failings of the weak, and not to please ourselves."* This makes us Jesus-like. The strong cannot exploit the weak nor take advantage of them.

The weak become the burden of the strong. The strong assume their responsibility and bear the burdens. You see, we act like Jesus. Jesus acted like the Father. We are taking Jesus's place in this old struggle.

How deeply important it is that this eternal life teaching should have its proper place.

First John 5:4 tells us, *"Whatever is born of God overcomes the world."* The overcomer belongs to the twice-born class.

One cannot be a failure when he knows that he has God's nature, knows his privileges in Christ, knows the authority of the name of Jesus, knows that God's strength is his, and knows that God's ability and wisdom are his. No matter what the opposition or the circumstances may be, he rises above them all.

Perhaps one of the most outstanding features of eternal life is that it permits us to go into the Father's presence at any time with the same freedom that Jesus had.

Hebrews 4:16 says, "*Come boldly to the throne of grace.*" The throne on which Jesus is seated is a grace throne. The word *grace* here means "love gifts." What a beautiful title: the throne of love gifts! I can come into His presence at any time.

In the morning when I awaken in His presence, I whisper, "Good morning, Father. Thank You for caring for me and for watching over me during the night. Good morning, Jesus. It is so beautiful of You to ever live to make intercession for me and to hold me in the embrace of Your faith and love."

There is a sweet intimacy between the Father and His children that is shown in Jesus's great high priestly prayer in John 17:23: "*That the world may know that You have sent Me, and have loved them as You have loved Me.*"

The weakest child has love's privilege granted to him. He may hide from the turmoil of the world in the throne room with his Father.

No more beautiful thing was ever spoken from the lips of Jesus than the words recorded in John 14:23: "*If anyone loves Me, he will keep My word; and My Father will love him, and We will come to him and make Our home with him.*"

There is a sweet, divine intimacy offered to us. No one can overestimate what it could mean to have the Father and Jesus in the home. What an effect it would have on the children! What an effect it would have upon the father and mother! No cross word would ever be spoken. There would be no bitter arguments. Love would be the first law of the home.

How divinely beautiful is the home life pictured by Jesus.

Isaiah 41:10 is a New Testament picture of the believer in his daily life:

> *Fear not, for I am with you; be not dismayed, for I am your God. I will strengthen you, yes, I will help you, I will uphold you with My righteous right hand.*

This Scripture is particularly precious. He is whispering to us in our daily walk. In the morning before we go to the office or our place of employment, we hear, "Do not fear. I will go with you. I will go ahead of you. I will prepare everything for your coming. I will watch over you today. My eye of love is upon you. No circumstance shall imprison or intimidate you today. My grace is all that you need. I am the strength of your life. I am your ability at every crisis. I am your God."

I love to think of Him as my Father-God. No Father ever loved his child as He loves you and me. No one ever planned for his child as His love has planned for us.

Every one of us has his place in the Father's love and in the Father's dreams. And when He whispers, "I am your Father-God," there is fragrance in it sweeter than violets or roses.

It is the fragrance of my Father's love. And He wants me to know that He cares for me, that my burdens are His. He wants me to cast every anxiety upon Him. Isn't that beautiful? This is the most attractive feature of this divine life.

He says, "Be not dismayed, for I am your Father-God."

Bills may come. Sickness may steal into your home, but you are a master. You and the Father are tied up together. He is greater than disease. He is greater than bills. He is greater than any irritation that can come into the home life.

He is your Father-God.

Jesus has become to you His right arm of righteousness. That is what a mother whispered about her son: "You know, he has become the right arm in our home."

He knew what she meant. He supported her; he watched over her. The son's love for his mother made him a safekeeper of his mother.

Jesus is the right arm of your righteousness. Love grows very bold with the Father in the house.

Eternal life, gaining the ascendancy over our natural human life, swallows it up after a while. We become immersed in it. Just as the Holy Spirit filled that upper room and immersed the disciples and made their spirits one with God, so now the Holy Spirit overshadows us and immerses us in His eternal life.

We have the strength of God awaiting us at every issue. We have the mind of Christ always available. We have the grace of our Lord Jesus and the love of the Father always available. How rich we are! We are led unconsciously into a quiet faith in Him.

In his letter to the Philippians, Paul writes:

I have learned in whatever state I am, to be content: I know how to be abased [live humbly], *and I know how to abound* [live in prosperity]. *Everywhere and in all things I have learned both to be full and to be hungry, both to abound and to suffer need. I can do all things through Christ who strengthens me.* (Philippians 4:11–13)

What a victorious, beautiful picture this is! It is what eternal life does for us in our daily walk. It gives us God's ability to face every problem of home and business, of social or political life.

SOME LOVE REALITIES

Eternal life makes new creations out of us. Perhaps, more accurately speaking, it forms a new creation in us.

We become a new type, a new species. God's very nature comes into our spirits, absorbing them, taking us over, and building into us the things that we saw and admired in Jesus. It gives us a sense of righteousness and freedom in the Father's presence.

No one can estimate the value of this unless they have known about the long struggles of men through the ages to rid themselves of sin consciousness. This sin consciousness has given us an inferiority complex. It has given birth to all the human religions and the vain reasonings of philosophy.

When one has received eternal life, he no longer has use for philosophy or religion. He has found reality. He has found the Father. Jesus has become a reality in his life.

He goes into the Father's presence now as simply and freely as a child goes into his earthly father's presence. Just as children flocked about Jesus in His earth walk, so we who have received eternal life crowd about the Father, longing for the closest, sweetest contact with Him.

It not only makes us new creations and makes us righteous, but it also imparts to us the love nature of the Father.

The greatest need in the world today is this Jesus kind of love. It will stop quarrelling and bitterness in the home. It will destroy the strife between the classes. It will bring joy and happiness wherever it goes. It is God working in the human spirit.

We no longer seek our own. Selfishness is destroyed. Speaking of love, 1 Corinthians 13:5 says it *"does not seek its own."* The thing that has motivated humanity down through the ages has been destroyed and another mighty force has taken its place. Selfishness has lost its crown. Love has taken the throne.

Another wonderful thing that eternal life gives us is wisdom. It is the ability to use the knowledge of our redemption from Satan, the knowledge of our righteousness, the knowledge of our standing with the Father, and how to use the name of Jesus that is given to us.

Wisdom is the ability to use all that God has given us in His grace. Wisdom is the master workman, the architect, the planner, and the designer of the human being.

This wisdom is ours. Jesus was made unto us wisdom from God. We cannot understand it. We just enjoy it and use it.

Would it not be wonderful if the church could learn to take advantage of this miracle-working ability that is in them? Let us begin to enjoy our rights, use this indwelling ability of God to bless and help people.

8

SPIRITUAL FORCES

The mightiest forces in the world are spiritual. They are not electricity or dynamite, but the unseen and unheard powers of the Spirit.

It staggered me when I first saw this fact. A Spirit had created material things. That unseen ability had brought mountains, metals, trees, and flowers into being just by saying, *"Let there be"* (Genesis 1:3). Then I realized that spiritual forces are mightier than anything that our senses have ever realized.

We have never realized that words are more powerful than bombs and tanks, but they are. And spiritual forces are the greatest forces in the world.

God is a Spirit. Angels are spirits. Demons are spirits. Man is a spirit. He lives in the midst of spiritual forces. When his spirit becomes united with God, his combat with these spiritual forces as a believer should always be with the consciousness that they are conquered, dethroned powers.

They hold sway over man because he does not recognize the fact that he has been set free and dominion over demonic forces has been placed in his hands.

When Jesus arose from the dead, it was because He had conquered these demonic forces and stripped them of their authority; He had broken their dominion over the human spirit.

When Jesus sat down at the right hand of the Father, it was because this redemption had been consummated. Then the new creation came into being. Jesus gave the new creation a legal right to the use of His name.

He declared, *"All authority has been given to Me in heaven and on earth. Go therefore and make disciples of all the nations"* (Matthew 28:18–19).

He didn't say "make converts," but *"make disciples,"* that is students. He wanted men and women who would enter into their privileges and take their places as sons and daughters in the Family of God.

Jesus conquered Satan for us. His victory over the adversary was our victory. We are conquerors today because of what He did. We enter into this victory by grace. We do not have to do a thing but simply repeat the name of Jesus and demons are defeated.

We have never yet appreciated the fact that our enemy is defeated and that our fight is a faith fight. It is our taking for granted that Satan is defeated that makes us masters. It is acting on the Word as though it were true that makes victors.

We have lived in the realm of the senses so long, depending upon what we see and hear, that it is difficult for us to grasp the reality of the unseen.

SENSE KNOWLEDGE FAITH

Most of the faith that we see today is sense knowledge faith. It says what Thomas said when Jesus rose from the dead, and the other disciples saw Him:

> *Unless I see in His hands the print of the nails, and put my finger into the print of the nails, and put my hand into His side, I will not believe.* (John 20:25)

It says what the crowds that gathered around Jesus said: "Do some miracle that we may see and believe." (See John 6:30.) The miracles which Jesus performed did not produce real faith in the people. It was only sense-knowledge faith. Real faith requires no sight or feeling, only the Word.

Our combat today is a combat with the unseen forces. The weapons that we use are the Word, the sword of our recreated spirits, the name of Jesus that has *"all authority"* (Matthew 28:18) in heaven, earth, and hell, and the shield of faith.

The Word on our lips becomes a devastating power to the adversary. The solid front we put up indicates their impending doom and our victory. We are going against the forces of darkness as Jehoshaphat went out against the hosts that came against Israel. Jehoshaphat had neither sword nor javelin. All he did was to draw his people up in battle array and sing a song of victory. God destroyed their enemies. (See 2 Chronicles 20.)

It seems a foolish thing from a sense knowledge point of view for me to say when a person has a high fever, "Fever, in the name of Jesus Christ, leave that body." The medical world ridicules it, but it works. The fever instantly departs.

I stood in the presence of one suffering with epilepsy. He was having an attack. In the name of Jesus, I commanded that demon to leave the body. It never came back again. That person had suffered from that dread disease for many years. He was instantly healed. All I used was the name of Jesus on my lips.

Demons know they are defeated foes. When we know it too and act, we see the results immediately. It is a fearless confidence in the Word of the Lord that conquers without a fight.

Spiritual strength and courage are built up by an intelligent, persistent confession of what the Word declares. Faith grows by acting on the Word and confessing your place. Faith is a product of the human spirit, not of the reasoning faculties. When this human spirit comes into vital contact with eternal life and the living Word, faith grows and becomes masterful.

Spirituality is oneness with the Word. Power over demons is just as real as our power over any force in nature.

Man built that great Coulee Dam, which controls the Columbia River. Now they turn a small wheel, allow the tremendous power of that great river to flow down, strike the turbines, and generate electricity.

Man is a master. God has given us mastery over demons.

I have stood before the insane and have heard the demons speak out of their lips and say to me, "You can't cast me out." And I answered, "Hush. In the name of Jesus, come out of this woman or this man." They came out, and their minds were restored.

This life in us is the secret of success, the secret of faith. You learn to trust the God in you. You learn what He can do through you and what you can do through His indwelling ability. Dare to act on His Word as you do on the word of doctors or lawyers.

9

SOME ETERNAL LIFE REALITIES

Christianity is a biological miracle. Christianity is not a religion. It is the imparted life or nature of God in man. It is more than the forgiveness of sins or the pardon of transgressions. It is an actual recreation. It is God's recreation of man by the impartation of His own nature.

It is the destroying of one nature and supplanting with a new nature, God's nature.

In the world, we have several different kinds of life. We have metal life, vegetable life, animal life, and human life. Above these there is another kind of life—God's life. God is the Author of all life.

Between these different kinds of life, there is an impassable gulf. Between the vegetable life and the animal life, there is an unbridged chasm. Vegetable life cannot beget animal life, and animal life cannot beget vegetable life.

Between animal life and human life there is a chasm unbridged by science. Animals cannot beget human life, nor can human beings beget animals. This fact utterly destroys the Darwinian hypothesis of evolution.

Our study is about human life and God's life. There are two Greek words used in the New Testament that show the vital contrast between the two. One is *psuche* and the other is *zoe*. The first refers to human life; the second to eternal life.

It would be well to note that when God created man, He created him in His own image and likeness. (See Genesis 1:26.) Man belongs to the same class of being as God. He was created so that he could become a partaker of God's nature, so that he could become God's child.

God is a Spirit. His Son was always a Spirit without a physical body until the day that God planned that the Son should take a human body. The Son has had a human body ever since. As far as we know, He will have it eternally. The Son, by taking a human body, forever linked humanity with God, proving that God can partake of humanity just as much as humanity can partake of God.

If God has taken over a human body, then men can take on God's nature and God's Spirit. If Jesus is the union of Deity and humanity—the two forms of life mingling and becoming one—then man can partake of God's nature, God's very substance and being and become one in relationship with God.

Jesus said, *"I am the vine, you are the branches"* (John 15:5). Our religious writers have failed to grasp the significance of this. Think of the unrealized possibilities wrapped up in this fact: that a man can partake of God's nature and so become God's child by the act called the new birth or the new creation. Think of the effect God's nature can have upon man's spirit and intellect!

We understand that it is man's spirit that receives the nature of God. It is the part of man that is recreated. Man, being in God's class of being—an eternal being, a spirit being—can naturally receive God's life.

Let us notice Jesus's teaching in the Gospel of John. *"I have come that they may have life, and that they may have it more abundantly"* (John 10:10).

Man is to have an abundance of God's life. Jesus would not have said this unless He was intimating the possibility of man's life being what Paul tells us in 2 Corinthians 5:4 (RSV): *"For while we are still in this tent [body], we sigh with anxiety; not that we would be unclothed, but that we would be further clothed, so that what is mortal may be swallowed up by life."*

We do not know all that this can mean, but it is so suggestive—*"swallowed up,"* filled with God's life.

The incarnation is really a prophecy of a superman, a man who has partaken of the nature of God, who has become godlike because God's nature has gained the ascendancy in him, in the new creation.

Jesus says in Mark 9:23, *"All things are possible to him who believes."* In other words, if a man acted on the Word of God, it would throw the realm of the supernatural open to him. Matthew 19:26 tells us, *"With God all things are possible."* Jesus says that with faith, *"nothing will be impossible for you"* (Matthew 17:20).

Can't you see the limitless possibilities in this new creation? God is in you. You have received the nature of God, have become a partaker of His very Being, His substance, and His life.

Along with that, Philippians 2:13 says, *"For it is God who works in you both to will and to do for His good pleasure."*

Can't you see the vast possibilities of the fact that God is in man? When we yield ourselves to this inward life, we are actually yielding ourselves to the personality of God that has come into us.

John tells us, *"You are of God, little children, and ... He who is in you is greater than he who is in the world"* (1 John 4:4).

No natural man is equal with Satan. No man has the ability that Satan has. But God in you is greater than Satan who is operating as the god of this world. God in you is greater than the laws of nature that surround you.

We saw God in Christ hushing the storm on the Sea of Galilee. We saw God in Jesus enabling Him to walk on the waves of that turbulent sea. We saw God in Him multiplying the bread until five loaves and three fish fed five thousand people until the disciples took up twelve basketfuls of fragments—broken pieces of bread and fish—from those little fish and those five thin loaves. (See, respectively, Matthew 8:26; 14:25; 14:19–21.)

Can't you see the possibilities of God in an individual? God has not lost His Godhood. He is just the same today.

This study of eternal life leads us into the realm of the supernatural where man actually becomes a super being. Ephesians 3:20 tells us, *"Now to Him who is able to do exceedingly abundantly above all that we ask or think, according to the power* [or ability] *that works in us."* That is a plain statement of fact: God with His limitless ability is at work within us.

What can't we do?

Mortal man has lived under the dominion of sin consciousness, weakness, and sickness, with the fear of death always haunting him. God lifts the curtain here and lets man have a vision of what he can be in Christ in this present life.

John 1:4 says, *"In Him was life, and the life was the light of men."* Our teachers have utterly failed to see the significance of this Scripture. A new kind of ability comes into man when this light-giving life enters him in the new birth.

This is a fact: wherever men have received eternal life, the next generation of that people, whether it is Christian or not, receives something that makes it produce inventors, discoverers, students, scientists, and educators.

The intellectual renaissance of Germany followed Martin Luther's teaching of the new birth.

The mechanical renaissance in England followed the Wesleyan and Whitefield revivals.

No heathen nation has ever needed a patent or copyright law until Jesus Christ has been preached among them, until men receive eternal life. This is a biological fact of stunning importance.

"In Him was life," and that life is the illumination of the human intellect wherever it is found. That light shone in the darkness of sense knowledge. Sense knowledge tried to destroy this revelation knowledge, this eternal life knowledge, and the battle that the church fought and in which she gave her thousands of martyrs came about because of eternal life. Those martyrs had received revelation knowledge. The peoples who were persecuting them had nothing but *psuche* life and sense knowledge that had come to them through the five senses.

Sense knowledge has thrown the Word out of the public schools, but it cannot destroy it.

Eternal life is the greatest thing that has ever come to the human race. It is the genius of Christianity.

The churches have never majored in it. All they have preached is sin, repentance, and what they call *salvation*. There has been no consciousness of what redemption meant: that man had been freed from the dominion of Satan as Israel was freed from Egypt, and with *zoe*, the life of God had been given to man.

So man has two kinds of life, natural and eternal. It is not a problem of sin; it is a life problem. Christ settled the sin problem in His substitutionary work. When a man accepts Christ as Savior and confesses Him as Lord, he receives eternal life at that moment. All he has ever done is remitted, and what he was stops being. He has passed into the realm of life.

> *Most assuredly, I say to you, he who hears My word and believes in Him who sent Me has everlasting life, and shall not come into judgment, but has passed from death into life.*
>
> (John 5:24)

The death mentioned here is spiritual death, which is the nature of God's enemy. It is just as much a reality as eternal life is. One is the nature of Satan; the other is the nature of God. Both of these natures are eternal. Neither can be destroyed. One produces hatred, ignorance, jealousy, bitterness, and murder. The other produces love, kindness, culture, refinement, happiness, and creative ability.

John 6:47 (RSV) says, "*Truly, truly, I say to you, he who believes has eternal life.*" That is, he who acts on the Word of God becomes a partaker of the life and nature of God. The object of redemption was that man might have eternal life.

And this is the testimony: that God has given us eternal life, and this life is in His Son. He who has the Son has life; he who does not have the Son of God does not have life. These things I have written to you who believe in the name of the Son of God, that you may know that you have eternal life.

(1 John 5:11–13)

John 5:26 says, "*For as the Father has life in Himself, so He has granted the Son to have life in Himself.*" That life is *zoe*, the new kind of life.

Jesus's earth walk perfectly illustrates the believer's earth walk. Jesus had eternal life abundantly in His earth walk, indicating that we who believe in Him and receive eternal life may have it abundantly even as He had it.

This Scripture adds light to this:

We know that we have passed from death to life, because we love the brethren. He who does not love his brother abides in death. Whoever hates his brother is a murderer, and you know that no murderer has eternal life abiding in him.

(1 John 3:14–15)

This combined with 1 John 4:7–8 explains the reality of Christianity: *"Beloved, let us love one another, for love is of God; and everyone who loves is born of God and knows God. He who does not love does not know God, for God is love."*

Love is the proof of God's nature having come unto us. Until a man receives God's nature, he will not love. He will have natural, human love, but he will not have the Jesus kind of love, the new kind of love that Jesus brought to the world.

The most impressive thing connected with Christianity was the new kind of love that men possessed.

Calvary illustrates it.

The disciples who gave up their lives proved that they possessed it. They loved men so mightily that no matter what was done to them, their love still governed their conduct.

Romans 5:12–21 (WNT) is very suggestive. It is the contrast of natural man with human life and the supernatural man with God's life. The 17th verse reads, *"For if, through the transgression of the one individual, Death made use of the one individual to seize the sovereignty, all the more shall those who receive God's overflowing grace and gift of righteousness reign as kings in Life through the one individual, Jesus Christ."*

Spiritual death seized the sovereignty when Adam sinned in the garden. Spiritual death is Satan's nature. Satan gained the mastery over man when Adam received that nature from him. Adam became spiritually united with Satan.

Not until Jesus came was there any deliverance from that awful sovereignty of spiritual death. But now, *"those who receive God's overflowing grace and the gift of righteousness reign as kings"* in the realm of eternal life.

Spiritual death is destroyed in the new creation. The new creation reigns as king, but he does not know it.

Eternal life makes men dominant beings. We are living in the infancy of this knowledge. It is so utterly new that the most advanced Christian thinkers are afraid of it. Yet here it is plainly given in the Word.

> *He has delivered us from the power of darkness [that is the darkness of spiritual death] and conveyed us into the kingdom of the Son of His love, in whom we have redemption through His blood, the forgiveness of sins.*
> (Colossians 1:13–14)

That brings us into the actual family of God. It takes us out of the family of Satan.

First John 3:10 says, *"In this the children of God and the children of the devil are manifest: Whoever does not practice righteousness is not of God, nor is he who does not love his brother."* The children of the adversary are dominated by spiritual death. The children of God are dominated by eternal life.

In the Gospel of John, Jesus gives us a new commandment:

> *A new commandment I give to you, that you love one another; as I have loved you, that you also love one another. By this all will know that you are My disciples, if you have love for one another.* (John 13:34–35)

The word for "love" here is *agape*. It is the new kind of love that springs out of a new kind of nature that has been given to the new creation. Man has something beyond confirmation, baptism, repentance, and forgiveness of sins. He has received eternal life.

If God had redeemed us out of the hand of the enemy but had not given us eternal life, we would be simply redeemed children of the devil with no ability to live the redeemed life.

In our redemption, there was a legal right given to us to receive eternal life. The moment we confess Jesus as Savior and Lord and believe in our hearts that God raised Him from the dead, eternal life is ours.

Forgiveness and righteousness given to us would be of no value until we received eternal life.

> *For by grace you have been saved through faith, and that not of yourselves; it is the gift of God, not of works, lest anyone should boast. For we are His workmanship, created in Christ Jesus for good works, which God prepared beforehand that we should walk in them.* (Ephesians 2:8–10)

We have been created in Christ Jesus in the mind of God. Now I accept Christ as my Savior and confess Him as my Lord, and the thing that God wrought in Christ becomes a reality in me. I have received the nature and life of God. I am now His child.

Receiving eternal life recreates our spirits, but our minds still receive all their impulses and knowledge through the avenue of the senses. This mind must be renewed, and the senses, the physical body, must be brought into subjection.

All the teaching about sanctification in Paul's epistles has reference to this fact: bringing the body into subjection to the Word of God.

He told the Romans, *"And do not be conformed to this world, but be transformed by the renewing of your mind, that you may prove what is that good and acceptable and perfect will of God"* (Romans 12:2).

The reason that faith is so weak is because of the lack of renewed minds. Until the mind is renewed, there will be no healthy, vigorous faith. These Scriptures show us what this renewed mind can be:

> *Be renewed in the spirit of your mind, and that you put on the new man which was created according to God, in true righteousness and holiness.* (Ephesians 4:23–24)

> For this reason we also, since the day we heard it, do not cease to pray for you, and to ask that you may be filled with the knowledge of His will in all wisdom and spiritual understanding; that you may walk worthy of the Lord, fully pleasing Him, being fruitful in every good work and increasing in the knowledge of God.   (Colossians 1:9–10)

The natural man cannot understand the things of God. That is why the first eight chapters of Romans were written in the realm of sense knowledge.

> But the natural man does not receive the things of the Spirit of God, for they are foolishness to him; nor can he know them, because they are spiritually discerned.   (1 Corinthians 2:14)

It is revelation, but it is a revelation unveiling the finished work of Christ to the man who walks according to the senses. Romans 8:1–12 shows the contrast between the man who walks in the senses and the man who walks in the spirit—that is, in this recreated spirit.

The renewed mind will be illumined by the Holy Spirit until the Word becomes a living reality, and we will be able to act and walk in the realm of our recreated spirits.

James 1:22 tells us that our actions must correspond with our faith. This renewed mind grasps the significance of this and enters into it.

James asks, *"What good is it, my brethren, if a man professes to have faith, and yet his actions do not correspond?"* (James 2:14 WNT).

The confession must be followed with acts that correspond to it. There is no real faith without this. If one believes, he will act on the Word he says he believes.

10

ETERNAL LIFE GIVES LOVE

The Word has taught us that love is the greatest thing in the world. As we study the life of Jesus, we find that He was not love conscious. He never saw the need for love in Himself because He *is* love.

We are the children of love. God, our Father, is love. We are partakers of His love nature. We are to live in love, to speak in love, and to act in love. Men are to feel Jesus in us. They are to see the Father in us.

Jesus said, "*He who has seen Me has seen the Father*" (John 14:9). We can say the same thing: "He who has seen me has seen love."

We are lovers. We walk in love. We speak in love. We think of men in terms of love. We have no conscious selfishness. We do not desire to use men for our own needs. We do not care to have money to gratify our own desires. We live as the Master lives—to love, to serve, and to give that others may be blessed because we have lived.

How rich and beautiful life becomes as love holds the reins, as love guides our lives! How beautiful is this way, this new and living way that Jesus opened up! It is the love way, the way of blessing and comfort and joy.

We have become one with Jesus. Can't you hear Him? He says, "I am the vine, and you are the branches. I am the love vine, and I am bearing love fruit through you."

In Galatians 5:22–23, Paul speaks of the fruit of the Spirit: *"But the fruit of the Spirit is love, joy, peace, longsuffering, kindness, goodness, faithfulness, gentleness, self-control. Against such there is no law."*

He is speaking of the recreated human spirit. The Holy Spirit only bears fruit through the recreated spirits. The first fruit that grows on that recreated branch is love. We are bearing love fruit, love deeds, love words, and love prayers.

We are taking over the infirmities of the weak as our own. We are bearing their burdens. We are carrying their loads. We are buying clothes for them if they are in need. We are meeting their needs. We are ministering to them. It is love's opportunity, love's way of living.

Love does not think evil thoughts. Love puts others first. Love never repeats scandal. It covers the mistakes and the failings of others with silence. *"Love never fails"* (1 Corinthians 13:8).

Love leads us on down through life with blessing, pouring out its fragrance as the rose pours out its perfume upon the air. The rose gives until finally the little petals are carried away on the bosom of the wind, and there is nothing left but the naked stem where once love's gorgeous beauty held court.

We will live like that.

The rose is all unconscious of it. It was a rose, and because it was a rose, it gave.

We are the children of love, and because we are the children of love, we give. This is the effect of eternal life, God's nature, imparted to men.

We have God's love nature in us. We are yielding ourselves to its sway. It has brought into our lives a new kind of joy and happiness that we never knew. This life is the Father's will for us. Jesus lived in the Father's will. So will we.

BEARING LOVE FRUIT

The vine does not bear fruit. It is the branch that bears it. Our recreated human spirits are the branches.

> *But the fruit of the Spirit is love, joy, peace, longsuffering, kindness, goodness, faithfulness, gentleness, self-control. Against such there is no law.* (Galatians 5:22–23)

We will notice just two or three of these fruits.

It helped me greatly when I saw that love is not the fruit of the human mind, but of the human spirit.

Romans 5:5 says, *"The love of God has been poured out in our hearts by the Holy Spirit who was given to us."* Here, the word *heart* is used synonymously with the word *spirit*. The Holy Spirit has shed abroad the Father's nature in our spirits. Now we bear the fruitage of love.

Faith also is the fruit of the recreated human spirit. Faith and love are not the fruits of our human intellects or reasoning faculties.

Jesus is *"the author and the finisher of our faith"* (Hebrews 12:2). His nature is imparted to our spirits and gives us His faith.

How it thrilled me when I discovered that all the things that the natural man craves are ours in Christ.

Man has craved faith. God is a faith God; Jesus is the faith Christ. We have their nature, so we have faith in us, and as we act on the Word, we see its fruits.

Jesus told the Jews that they must have faith for their healing and for the other things they craved. All those things belong to us; they are in our redemption.

The Lord never tells us in any of the Epistles, "You must believe to get your healing," "You must believe in order to get money," or "You must believe in order to get strength." These are all ours in the new creation.

WISDOM IS ABILITY TO USE HIS KNOWLEDGE

Wisdom is given to us in Christ. It is something that comes down from above, a supernatural gift to our recreated spirits in Christ. First Corinthians 1:30 says, *"But of Him you are in Christ Jesus, who became for us wisdom from God."* This ability to use knowledge is ours for daily use.

James tells the *babes* in Christ, *"If any of you lacks wisdom, let him ask of God, who gives to all liberally and without reproach, and it will be given to him. But let him ask in faith, with no doubting"* (James 1:5–6). Paul, writing to the mature believers, says Jesus became wisdom from God for us.

James asks, *"Is anyone among you sick? Let him call for the elders of the church"* (James 5:14). There should not be any sick among us. We ought to know that Christ was made sick for us. All we need to do is to enjoy our health in Christ.

But the babes in Christ, the men and women who have been living beneath their privileges, who have never developed their spirits, are living in the realm of the senses rather than in the realm of the Word.

To those who have received eternal life but have never grown in grace and knowledge, Paul writes:

> *For though by this time you ought to be teachers, you need some one to teach you again the first principles of God's word.*
>
> (Hebrews 5:12 RSV)

These people have never taken advantage of their privileges. They are still babes in Christ. In his first letter to the Corinthians, Paul writes:

> *And I, brethren, could not speak to you as to spiritual people but as to carnal, as to babes in Christ. I fed you with milk and not with solid food; for until now you were not able to receive it, and even now you are still not able; for you are still carnal. For where there are envy, strife, and divisions among you, are you not carnal and behaving like mere men?*
>
> (1 Corinthians 3:1–3)

The word *carnal* means "sense governed." These babes in Christ have never grown out of their first faith in Christ as Savior. The vast riches of grace that belong to them have never been touched. They have eternal life, but they are living under the direction of their senses. It is what they see, what they feel, and what they experience that governs their lives. The Word has not yet gained the ascendancy over them.

They must have others pray for them because they can't take their rights. They know nothing of the Word.

The senses are active competitors of the Word. They war against the Word. They keep the recreated spirit in bondage until the mind is renewed.

Treat the Word as you would treat the Master if He were here. Act on the Word as you would on a direct message from Jesus.

11

WHEN WAS ETERNAL LIFE FIRST GIVEN TO MAN?

Could eternal life be given to man before sin was put away? There is more confusion in the minds of believers in regard to this than perhaps to almost any other great teaching in the Word.

Hebrews 9:26 says, "*But now, once at the end of the ages, He [Jesus] has appeared to put away sin by the sacrifice of Himself.*"

The two ages—the old covenant and the new one—met at the cross. The new covenant came into actual being on the day of Pentecost. The old covenant died when the new covenant became a reality. The law of the old covenant stopped functioning, and the law of the new covenant began.

The old priesthood—with its sacrifices, the blood atonement, and the scapegoat—no longer functioned in the mind of God. Jesus as the Lamb of God had dealt with the sin and the sinner problem.

The Hebrew word for *atonement* means "to cover" or a "covering." The word *atonement* does not occur in the Greek. Romans 5:11 refers to reconciliation, not atonement.

Spiritually dead Israel was covered with the blood of bulls and goats once a year, and the sins that they had committed that year were borne away on the head of the scapegoat.

God dealt with the sin nature and the things it had caused them to do. The men of the old covenant were "under the blood" because of the life that was in the blood.

Leviticus 17:11 (RSV) explains, *"For the life of the flesh is in the blood; and I have given it for you upon the altar to make atonement for your souls; for it is the blood that makes atonement, by reason of the life."*

Israel was spiritually dead. Had they been made alive in spirit, they would have needed no covering.

The believer is not covered with the blood of Christ but is cleansed by it. When a man is born again, he receives the life and nature of God. No one was born again until the day of Pentecost. He couldn't be because the sin problem had never been settled.

Jesus said, *"I have come that they may have life, and that they may have it more abundantly"* (John 10:10).

> *Is the law then against the promises of God? Certainly not! For if there had been a law given which could have given life, truly righteousness would have been by the law.*
> (Galatians 3:21)

The Scripture shut up all things under sin; that is, all had sinned and fallen short of God's demands.

Israel was blood-covered once a year. They had no eternal life. They had no righteousness. They had a righteousness if they kept the law, but because they couldn't keep the law, God protected them by the atoning blood. The law became the Jew's tutor until Christ, that the Jew might be justified by faith. Now faith is come, and the Jew is no longer under a tutor. Now he can accept Jesus Christ as a Savior and become a son.

You will notice that there are two things here that the first covenant could not give. It could not give eternal life, and it could not make man righteous. It could reckon righteousness unto a man, but it could not impart righteousness to him.

Eternal life was promised him, but he was still spiritually dead. We can see that sin and sins had to be dealt with before man could receive eternal life.

Jesus dealt with the sin problem in His redemptive work. He conquered Satan and rose from the dead to justify us before the court of justice.

SOME FACTS ABOUT JESUS

Colossians 1:18 says Jesus was *"the firstborn from the dead."* He was born out of spiritual death.

In Acts 13:30–33 and Hebrews 1:5–6, the Father speaks of His risen Son: *"You are My Son, today I have begotten You."* This was when Jesus was made alive in spirit before His resurrection.

So Jesus was *"the firstborn among many brethren"* (Romans 8:29).

12

THE REIGN OF ETERNAL LIFE

We read in Romans 5:17 (WNT):

> *For if, through the transgression of the one individual, Death made use of the one individual to seize the sovereignty, all the more shall those who receive God's overflowing grace and gift of righteousness reign as kings in Life through the one individual, Jesus Christ.*

Here is the story of Satan's seizure of man's dominion in the garden, when he changed man's spirit nature, made his body mortal, and made that body the master of his spirit.

Man became the servant of the senses; his spirit no longer ruled him. Man's spirit became subject to Satan's nature: spiritual death. In this we witness the tragedy of love. God's love creation became the slave of hate.

> *Then God said, "Let Us make man in Our image, according to Our likeness; let them have dominion over the fish of the sea, over the birds of the air, and over the cattle, over all the earth and over every creeping thing that creeps on the earth."*
> (Genesis 1:26)

Study this with Psalm 8:3–6:

When I consider Your heavens, the work of Your fingers, the moon and the stars, which You have ordained, what is man that You are mindful of him, and the son of man that You visit him? For You have made him a little lower than the angels, and You have crowned him with glory and honor. You have made him to have dominion over the works of Your hands; You have put all things under his feet.

This is a picture of God's man in the garden before sin came.

Consider also these verses from Hebrews:

For He has not put the world to come, of which we speak, in subjection to angels. But one testified in a certain place, saying: "What is man that You are mindful of him, or the son of man that You take care of him? You have made him a little lower than the angels; You have crowned him with glory and honor, and set him over the works of Your hands. You have put all things in subjection under his feet. (Hebrews 2:5–8)

This vast authority, this great honor God had conferred upon man, was turned over into the hands of the adversary. Man became the subject of Satan.

He had been God's under-ruler. What a wonderful being he must have been with a mind so capable that he named the entire animal and vegetable creation, with a dominion so vast that the very heavens were subject to him! Then he fell under the dominion of Satan.

We can now understand Romans 5:17. Satan seized the sovereignty. He became the lord and head of man. He became the god of this world. He became the spiritual father of the human race. Politically he became the prince of this world.

Down through the ages, we have seen the reign of spiritual death. Satan's nature is death, just as God's nature is life. The first manifestation of the satanic nature is hatred. Hatred, selfishness, bitterness, and murder are the dominant features of Satan's dominion.

The reign of spiritual death is the reign of Satan. It is sin that rules in the realm of spiritual death. Sin is organized evil.

Man has become the servile subject of the devil. He has no revelation knowledge, so he is utterly dependent upon the knowledge he derives through his senses. His body has become his master.

Into this maelstrom of hatred and sorrow, tears and anguish, the Son of God was born. *"And the Word became flesh and dwelt among us"* (John 1:14). Love was manifested in the flesh. It was love's intrusion. It was God breaking into Satan's dominion.

Then they crucified love. They nailed it to the cross. But love arose from the dead.

Did you ever notice this Scripture? *"God was manifested in the flesh, justified in the Spirit"* (1 Timothy 3:16). God is describing His Son as a substitute after He had left His body and gone to the place of suffering.

God had laid upon Him our sins and diseases. God had made Him to be sin that we might be His righteousness in Christ. He stayed there until He had satisfied every claim of justice. Then He was justified in spirit.

> *For Christ also died for sins once for all, the righteous for the unrighteous, that he might bring us to God, being put to death in the flesh but made alive in the spirit.* (1 Peter 3:18 RSV)

This is not referring to the Holy Spirit, but to Christ's spirit. He had died spiritually. He had become a partaker of the satanic nature on the cross. When God laid our sin upon Him, He became sin. He had never known sin, but He became identified with Satan.

His body became mortal so that He could die. He could not have died physically unless He had died spiritually.

I lay down My life that I may take it again. No one takes it from Me, but I lay it down of Myself. I have power to lay it down, and I have power to take it again. (John 10:17–18)

Jesus could not have died until His body had become mortal. This could not have been until He was made sin. Then He was justified, declared righteous, and given eternal life. *"He is the head of the body, the church, who is the beginning, the firstborn from the dead"* (Colossians 1:18).

Jesus was the first person ever born again. Out of that new birth, the church was born. *"For we are His workmanship, created in Christ Jesus"* (Ephesians 2:10).

"You are My Son, today I have begotten You" (Acts 13:33). This has reference to His resurrection. Then Jesus stripped Satan of his authority, conquered him, and arose from the dead. The reign of the new life began.

It is important that we understand the teaching of identification. Read my book *Identification*.[1] Paul teaches us in this great revelation that we were crucified with Christ, died with Christ, were buried with Christ, suffered with Christ, were made alive together with Christ, were justified with Christ, were raised together with Christ, and then were seated together with Him at the right hand of God. This is the mystery of substitution.

Jesus was our substitute. It was the same as though we had been nailed to the cross with Him, had died with Him, had been buried with Him, had suffered with Him, had conquered Satan with Him, had been justified with Him, had been made alive with Him, had arisen with Him, and were seated with Him.

---

1. E. W. Kenyon, *Identification: A Romance in Redemption* (New Kensington, PA: Whitaker House, 2021).

His victory over Satan was real. What He did, He did for us. What He is, He is for us.

He is the firstborn of the church. As our substitute, He conquered Satan and stripped him of his authority. He did it in our stead. We were credited with that victory. God sees us as He has made us in Christ.

So the Spirit can say through Paul that we reign as kings in the realm of life through Jesus Christ, our Lord. We are Satan's masters. We reign over him. Today, as sons of God, we are masters of our old enemy. It is the *"abundance of grace"* and *"the gift of righteousness"* (Romans 5:17). It is the reign of righteousness.

We must learn to see ourselves as the Father sees us in Christ, as victors in every field.

Don't take Satan's estimation of yourself. This is the reign of those whom God calls His *righteous ones* in Christ. Hebrews 10:38 (RSV) says, *"My righteous one shall live by faith."* We are those righteous ones.

This new creation is enthroned with Christ. We are seated with Him in the heavenlies.

The new creation is master of the adversary. The old creation was a failure. The new creation is a success.

We have the very nature and life of God that makes us righteous. It gives us access to the very throne of God. We can go into the throne room just as Jesus did in His earth walk. I was almost tempted to say, "As a child goes into his father's room without knocking." A stranger wouldn't dare to do it.

We have a legal right to the use of the name of Jesus. He has given us the power of attorney to use it. He said, *"All authority has been given to Me in heaven and on earth"* (Matthew 28:18). And He said, *"Whatever you ask the Father in My name He will give you"*

(John 16:23). This is dominion over the adversary. This is mastery over demonic forces and their works.

Now 1 John 4:4 is a reality: *"You are of God, little children."* We are born of God. We have overcome the evil one. Why? Because *"He who is in you* [God] *is greater than he* [Satan] *who is in the world."*

Satan knows we are masters. His success depends on keeping us in ignorance of this fact. He knows that we will make mistakes, so he uses our mistakes to keep us under condemnation.

The church has never recognized the ministry of Jesus at the right hand of the Father. He is there as our Advocate, our heavenly lawyer. First John 2:1 explains, *"And if anyone sins, we have an Advocate with the Father, Jesus Christ the righteous."* All we need to do is to whisper, "Father, in Jesus's name, forgive me for that foolish thing I have said." At once, our fellowship with the Father is restored.

Satan knows that we are taking Jesus's place in the world. He wants to keep us ignorant of it. It gives us strength and courage when we read Matthew 28:20: *"And lo, I am with you always, even to the end of the age."*

If He is with us, we are afraid of nothing.

If God is for us, who can be against us? He who did not spare His own Son, but delivered Him up for us all, how shall He not with Him also freely give us all things?
(Romans 8:31–32)

Can't you hear Him say in the next verses:

Who shall bring a charge against God's elect? It is God who justifies. Who is he who condemns? It is Christ who died, and furthermore is also risen, who is even at the right hand of God, who also makes intercession for us.   (Romans 8:33–34)

What a standing we have before the very throne of God! What recognition we have from the Father Himself! What limitless ability is ours!

Shall we live on in ignorance of our rights? Let us study His Word until we know what is ours in Him. Faith comes with the knowledge of our rights in Christ.

When you act on the knowledge of what you are in Christ, you glorify the Son and make the Father's heart glad. Say it over and over, "I am what He says I am; I can do what He says I can do. He will do in me all He did in Christ for me. I have His nature in me—His love nature, His creative nature, His faith nature. I am His very child. All things are possible to the believing one. I am a believer, so it is I of whom He speaks."

Three blessed facts that have never been stressed:

1. What God really did for us in Christ in His great redemptive work.

2. What God does for us in the new creation, through the Word and by the Holy Spirit, building His nature into us and making us like Jesus in our love walk.

3. What Jesus is doing now for us at God's right hand as Mediator for the lost, as High Priest for the believer, as surety for the new covenant, as the Advocate for us when tempted, and as our Lord and Sustainer.

13

RIGHT AND WRONG CONFESSIONS

New Christians have recognized the place that confession holds in the scheme of things. Whenever the word *confession* is used, we instinctively think of confessing sin, weakness, and failure. That is the negative side of this question.

Christianity is called the *great confession*. Confessing is affirming something that we believe. It is testifying of something that we know. It is witnessing for a truth that we have embraced. Confession holds a very large place in Christianity.

Jesus planned that this great life and love should be given to the world through testimony—that is, through the confession of our lips. Testifiers, witnesses, and confessors have been the great leaders in the revolutionary life that Jesus gave to the world. The major problem that we face, then, is to know what we are to confess.

Our confession centers around several things:

- First, what God in Christ has wrought for us.
- Second, what God through the Word and the Spirit has wrought in us.

- Third, what we are to the Father in Christ.
- And last of all, what God can do through us, or what the Word will do on our lips.

You cannot confess or witness about things you do not know. It is what you have seen and heard that counts in the courtroom. It is what you know personally about Jesus Christ and about what you are in Christ that counts in life. How few of us dare to confess to the world what the Word declares that we are in Christ!

Take this Scripture, for example: *"Therefore, if anyone is in Christ, he is a new creation"* (2 Corinthians 5:17). What a revolutionary thing it would be for the church to make a confession like that! They are not just forgiven sinners, not poor, weak, staggering, sinning church members. They are new creations created in Christ Jesus with the life of God, the nature of God, and the ability of God in them.

What a stir it would make in the modern church for you to confess that you are absolutely redeemed. It would mean that Satan's dominion has been broken; he lost his dominion over your life the moment you became a new creation. You received a new Lord, Jesus Christ, to reign over you.

> *In Him we have redemption through His blood, the forgiveness of sins, according to the riches of His grace which He made to abound toward us in all wisdom and prudence.*
> (Ephesians 1:7–8)

Satan's dominion ended and Jesus's dominion began. Disease and sickness can no longer lord it over you. The old habits can no longer lord it over you. You are a new creation, created in Christ.

What a stir there would be if this Scripture became a reality:

Fear not, for I am with you; be not dismayed, for I am your God. I will strengthen you, yes, I will help you, I will uphold you with My righteous right hand. (Isaiah 41:10)

"If God is for us, who can be against us?" (Romans 8:31). This is the most revolutionary thing that has ever been taught. It is your confession as you stand before the world. "God is with me this morning."

You are of God, little children, and have overcome them, because He who is in you is greater than he who is in the world. (1 John 4:4)

You fearlessly say, "God is in me now. The Master of creation is in me!" What a confession that is! You face life fearlessly. You know now that greater is He who is in you than all the forces that can be arrayed against you.

You are facing bills that you cannot pay. You are facing enemies that you have no ability to conquer, and yet you face them fearlessly. You say with triumph, "He prepares a table before me in the presence of my enemies, and He anoints my head with oil." (See Psalm 23:5.)

I am filled with joy and victory because God has taken me over; He is fighting my battles. I am not afraid of circumstances because *"I can do all things through Christ who strengthens me"* (Philippians 4:13).

He is not only my strength, but He is at my right hand. *"The Lord is my light and my salvation; whom shall I fear?"* (Psalm 27:1). He throws light upon life's problems so that I know I can act intelligently. He is my salvation, my deliverance from every trap that the enemy sets for me, from every snare in which he would enslave me.

God is the strength of my life, so why should I be afraid? I am not afraid of anything. I have no fear because this God of omnipotence is on my side. This is my continual confession.

I confess that I have a redemption that God planned and wrought in Christ. I am a new creation of which He, Himself, is the author and the finisher. (See Hebrews 12:2.)

I have a righteousness that permits me to stand in His presence as though sin had never been.

I not only have righteousness reckoned to me, but I have righteousness imparted to me in the new nature that I have received from Him. I have received His nature, His life, and in this life and nature is the life of God. This makes me righteous even as He is righteous.

This is my confession. This gives me boldness in prayer. This builds faith. This makes my way sure. I am no longer hemmed in by limitations because I am united with the limitless One.

He is the vine, and I am the branch. As a branch, I bear His fruit because the vine is imparting to me the fullness of His life. I know the reality of this because it has become a part of my very being.

I know I love because He has shed abroad His love in my heart through the Holy Spirit, and I know that His nature in me is love. His love ability has gained the mastery, for now I can love in whatever circumstances I am placed.

I can say with joy, "Sin shall not have dominion over me." (See Romans 6:14.) It can no longer lord itself over me. Circumstances can no longer hold me in bondage and hinder my usefulness in the world.

I not only have God's life in me and this great Spirit who raised Jesus up from the dead in me, but I have the use of Jesus's name.

He has given to me the legal right to use it. My confession is that whatever I ask of the Father in His name, He gives to me.

He has given me the power of attorney. I am using that power to help men. I am taking Jesus's place now. He is working His own work through me. He is living His own life in me.

Jesus said, *"In My name they will cast out demons"* (Mark 16:17). I am exercising my rights. He said, *"They will lay hands on the sick, and they will recover"* (verse 18). My hands become the medium through which His life pours. I am living the abundant life. I know my words are His words.

His words broke the power of death and demons; His words healed the sick. They do the same thing on my lips. This is my confession. This is my heart expressing itself through words on my lips.

Confession is faith's way of expressing itself. Faith, like love, is only revealed in action and word. There is no faith without confession. Faith grows with your confession.

Confession does several things to the believer. It locates him. It fixes the landmarks of his life. It mightily affects his spirit, the inner man, when he makes his declaration.

For instance, note these verses from Romans:

> *If you confess with your mouth the Lord Jesus and believe in your heart that God has raised Him from the dead, you will be saved. For with the heart one believes unto righteousness, and with the mouth confession is made unto salvation.*
> (Romans 10:9–10)

There are two confessions involved here. First, a confession of the lordship of Jesus. And second, that one has become the righteousness of God and is saved. These are positive confessions.

The reason that the majority of Christians are earnest yet weak is because they have never dared to make a confession of what they are in Christ. What they must do is to find what they are in the mind of the Father—how He looks upon them—and then confess it. This can be found in the Epistles.

When you find this, you boldly make your confession of what the Word declares you are in Christ. As you do this, your faith will abound.

The reason your faith is throttled and held in bondage is because you have never dared to confess what God says you are.

Remember, faith never grows beyond your confession. Your daily confession of what the Father is to you, what Jesus is now doing for you at the right hand of the Father, and what the mighty Holy Spirit is doing in you will build a positive, solid faith life. You will not be afraid of any circumstance, any disease, or any condition. You will fearlessly face life as a conqueror.

You will never be a conqueror until you confess it. After a while, you will find that Romans 8:37 is true: *"Yet in all these things we are more than conquerors through Him who loved us."*

A WRONG CONFESSION

A wrong confession is the confession of defeat, of failure, and of the supremacy of Satan. Talking about your combat with the devil, how he has hindered you, and how he is holding you in bondage and keeping you sick is a confession of defeat. It is a wrong confession. It glorifies your adversary. It is an unconscious declaration that your Father-God is a failure.

Most of the confessions that we hear today glorify the devil. Such a confession continually saps the very life out of you. It destroys faith and holds you in bondage.

The confession of your lips that has grown out of faith in your heart will absolutely defeat the adversary in every combat.

The confession of Satan's ability to hinder you and keep you from success gives Satan dominion over you and fills you with fear and weakness. But if you boldly confess your Father's care and protection and declare that He is in you and is greater than any force around you, you will rise above satanic influence.

Every time you confess your doubts and fears, you confess your faith in Satan and deny the ability and grace of God. When you confess your weakness and your disease, you are openly confessing that the Word of God is not true, and God has failed to make it good.

His Word declares, "With His stripes, you were healed," and "Surely He has borne your sicknesses and carried your diseases." (See Isaiah 53:4–5.)

Instead of confessing that He has borne my diseases and put them away, if I confess that I still have them, I am taking the testimony of my senses instead of the testimony of the Word of God. As long as I hold fast to my confession of weakness, sickness, and pain, I will still have them. I may search for years for some man of God to pray the prayer of faith for me, and it will be of no avail because my unbelief destroys the effect of his faith.

The believer who is always confessing his sins and his weakness is building weakness, failure, and sin into his consciousness. And yet:

> *If we confess our sins, He is faithful and just to forgive us our sins and to cleanse us from all unrighteousness.* (1 John 1:9)

When that confession has been made, we never refer to it again. It is not past history because history can be remembered. *This is as though it had never been.* We should never remind ourselves or the Lord of our failings or of our past mistakes. They are not!

If you confess anything, confess that you stand complete in Him. Confess that what God has said in regard to your mistakes and blunders is absolutely true.

We should never confess our sins to other people. We may have to ask them to forgive us, but then we are to forget it.

Never tell anyone about your weakness or about your past blunders and failures. They will not forget them; sometimes, they will remind you of them. If you tell it to anyone, tell it to the Lord and then forget it.

DARE TO MAKE YOUR CONFESSION

You confess that God is the Lord of your life, that He is the Lord over disease, sickness, and Satan. You hold fast to your confession of Jesus's absolute lordship over everything that would keep you in bondage or hinder you from enjoying the finished work of Christ.

In the face of every need, you confess, *"The Lord is my shepherd; I shall not want"* (Psalm 23:1). Always confess this in the present tense. He is your supply. He is your health and your strength. He is the strength of your life; of whom will you be afraid?

Remember that we never realize beyond our confession.

If you dare to confess healing on the ground of the Word, then there is no sickness for you. In the face of pain and an open sore, you confess that with His stripes, you are healed, and you hold fast to your confession, never wavering, knowing that no Word from God is void of power. (See Isaiah 55:11.)

God's Word has the ability to make good. That Word will heal you if you continually confess it. Your body will respond to your mind, and your spirit will gain the lordship over your body and mind. Your body will obey your confession.

"*He sent His word and healed them*" (Psalm 107:20). Jesus was that Word. Now that name of Jesus and the words of Jesus become your healing.

Confession is confirming the Word of God. It is a confession of my confidence in what God has spoken.

There are several confessions every believer should make:

> *If you confess with your mouth the Lord Jesus and believe in your heart that God has raised Him from the dead, you will be saved. For with the heart one believes unto righteousness, and with the mouth confession is made unto salvation.*
> (Romans 10:9–10)

We confess the absolute lordship of Jesus and the absolute righteousness that is imparted to us in our redemption. We dare to confess before the world and before the throne of God that Jesus is now our Lord and that we have received salvation and become the righteousness of God in Him.

We confess that we are new creations of which Jesus is the head and the Lord. The Word has taken Jesus's place in our lives. We are to obey the Word as we would obey Jesus if He stood in our presence.

A second confession is found in 1 Peter 5:7: "*Casting all your care upon Him, for He cares for you.*"

We confess that we no longer have cares, anxieties, and burdens. We can never have nervous prostration. We can never be unnerved and unfit from life's work. Our minds are complete and clear. Our spirits are free. Our testimony has the unction of the Spirit upon it because He bears every burden, carries every load, and meets every need.

A third confession is, "*The Lord is my shepherd; I shall not want*" (Psalm 23:1). I do not want for money, I do not want for health or rest. I do not want for strength. I do not want for anything. He is all that I need.

This is a living reality. What a life is mine! What a sense of security, of power, and of victory!

You are not afraid to take your stand on Philippians 4:19: "My God shall supply every need of mine."

You loudly make your fourth confession: that Isaiah 53:3–5 is true.

Every disease, every weakness, and every infirmity was laid on Jesus Christ, and you are free from them. Just as He bore your sin, He bore your disease. You stand complete in Him, free from the burden, the power, the pain, and the effect of disease. This confession gives you a healthy body, a clear mind, and a conquering spirit.

Your fifth confession is that 1 Corinthians 1:30 is absolutely true: *"But of Him you are in Christ Jesus, who became for us wisdom from God—and righteousness and sanctification and redemption."*

Christ has been made all these things to you. You do not need to pray for wisdom as James 1:5 tells the babes in Christ to do because He is your wisdom. You do not have to ask for righteousness because you have become the righteousness of God in Him. You don't have to ask Him to sanctify you because He is your sanctification. You do not have to pray for redemption because you are redeemed. He is your redemption.

What a confession to make before the world!

Hebrews 4:14 says, *"Let us hold fast our confession."*

We have found in a measure what our confession is, but there is a great deal more to it than you find in this book. Your success and usefulness in the world is going to be measured by your confession and by the tenacity with which you hold fast to that confession under all circumstances.

You absolutely refuse to yield or be stampeded by circumstances or the opinions of men. You will never yield to fear or listen to the voice of the senses. You stand by your confession, knowing that God cannot fail you.

There is a grave danger of a dual confession. You confess His faithfulness, the absolute truthfulness of His Word, yet at the same time, you confess your sickness. You confess your weakness, your lack of money, your lack of ability. You have confessed that He was your supply, that He was your healer. You have confessed that you were healed by His stripes. Now you talk about your lack of ability to do this or that because of your sickness.

You cannot do the housework or go about your business because you are not able to do it, yet you have made your confession that He was the strength of your life and that with His stripes, you were healed.

Your confession of sickness and disease destroys your faith. You are not holding fast to the confession of what you are in Christ, or what He is to you.

This is one of the most dangerous of all confessions. You will find that you have been so carefully trained in the confession of wrong, failure, weakness, sin, sickness, and want that it will take a great deal of discipline through the Word to cure you of the habit.

Now make your right confession and stand by it.

14

THE RENEWED MIND

We used to wonder why certain people grew in grace so much more rapidly than others and why the Bible became such an open revelation to them.

We thought that it came through prayer, surrender, and consecration, or through some new unusual experience. We thought that if we had the experience that many claimed in regard to the Holy Spirit, it would produce this result.

Then as we contacted people who made a specialty of teaching the ministry of the Holy Spirit, we found that even these leaders lacked insight in the Word and clearness of teaching.

We asked ourselves, "Where is the solution of this?"

As we searched the Epistles again—because we knew that it must be in Paul's revelation—we ran across a word that was new to us. We found it in Romans 12:2: "*And do not be conformed to this world, but be transformed* [or transfigured] *by the renewing of your mind, that you may prove what is that good and acceptable* [or well-pleasing] *and perfect will of God.*"

We notice first that there are three wills of the Father suggested here: the *good* will, the *acceptable* will, and the *perfect* will. For every life, there is a good will, a well-pleasing will, and His best will, the perfect will.

Here is a man who is born again. The part of him that is recreated is his spirit. Into his spirit has come the nature of the Father, but his mind is still the old mind that received its education through the senses. (Read my book, *The Two Kinds of Knowledge*.[2])

This mind is governed by the sense knowledge of the world. In other words, it is a world-ruled mind. It cannot seem to grasp spiritual things. Such a man is described in 1 Corinthians 2:14: "*But the natural man* [or mind] *does not receive the things of the Spirit of God, for they are foolishness to him; nor can he know them, because they are spiritually discerned.*"

This natural man or natural mind can understand material things, but it cannot grasp spiritual things. What can be done to it?

The spirit is recreated, and there does not seem to be any harmony between the recreated spirit and the unrenewed mind.

The mind must be renewed.

Man is a spirit being. When Adam sinned, he died spiritually. Spiritual death has governed man's thinking processes and has in a large measure governed his body.

As I have shown you, the new birth is a real birth or recreation of the spirit, which brings it into fellowship and harmony with the Father. Spiritual life is the nature of God that comes to us at the new birth. Spiritual death is the nature of Satan, which was imparted to man when he fell.

All men are spiritually dead and cannot stand in the Father's presence until they are recreated.

---

2. E. W. Kenyon, *The Two Kinds of Knowledge: God's Wisdom Is Greater Than Our Senses* (New Kensington, PA: Whitaker House, 2024).

Jesus was spiritually in union with the Father from His birth because He was conceived of the Holy Spirit. When He went to the cross, God laid upon Him our sin. Jesus then became a partaker of spiritual death. He died spiritually. His body became mortal the instant His Spirit underwent this transformation.

He took our sins, diseases, and our nature. He took our place and went to the prison house of suffering in our stead. He stayed in this place for three days and three nights. Then He was justified or declared righteous by the Father because He had satisfied the claims of justice.

The moment He was justified, He was made alive in spirit. It was then that God said, *"You are My Son, today I have begotten You"* (Acts 13:33). This was the new birth of Jesus. He then conquered the adversary and arose from the dead. His body then received immortality.

Before He went to the cross, He had a perfect human existence, a perfect human body over which death had no authority. He said, *"I lay down My life that I may take it again. No one takes it from Me, but I lay it down of Myself"* (John 10:17–18).

On the cross, He became mortal, a subject of death. When He arose from the dead, His body was immortal. With that immortal body, He sat down at the right hand of the Majesty on High. He is there now on our behalf.

When we accept Jesus Christ, we receive the same nature and life that Jesus did. We become partakers of the nature of God. The new birth is man's spirit being recreated by the nature of the Father. The mind is not born again, just the spirit. The process of renewing the mind is the great work of the ministry.

There are three important facts for us to notice: recreating the spirit; renewing the mind; and controlling the body or senses.

The first fact is found in Romans 3–6, where we read of the recreation of man's spirit. In that last chapter, we are told:

> *Therefore do not let sin reign in your mortal body, that you should obey it in its lusts. And do not present your members as instruments of unrighteousness to sin, but present yourselves to God as being alive from the dead, and your members as instruments of righteousness to God. For sin shall not have dominion over you.* (Romans 6:12–14)

Here He shows us the relation of the recreated spirit to our physical body or senses. Your spirit has been recreated. You live in the same kind of a body that you have always lived in. This body must be brought into subjection to the Word of God through your spirit.

Before that can be done, the truth brought out in Romans 12:1 must become a reality: *"Present your bodies a living sacrifice, holy, acceptable to God, which is your reasonable service."*

Our bodies are the universities through which our senses teach us sense knowledge. Your body, in most cases, rules your mind and spirit. So He tells us to have our minds renewed. (See Romans 12:2.)

If you are sick, the body instantly takes the ascendancy over the mind and the spirit. The mind has ruled the spirit in natural man almost entirely.

Conscience is the voice of your spirit. It is your spirit speaking out against certain things and approving of other things.

The moment you are born again, your spirit becomes the voice of a recreated spirit in fellowship with the Father. It becomes the vehicle through which God speaks to you.

Man's spirit is the point of contact between God and man, and between Satan and man in a very large measure.

The problem is that of renewing the mind to bring it into fellowship with a recreated spirit so that the two together can govern the body and bring it into subjection to the Word.

Galatians 5:18–19 shows the war of the senses against the recreated spirit:

> But if you are led by the Spirit, you are not under the law. Now the works of the flesh are evident, which are: adultery, fornication, uncleanness, lewdness.

The word *flesh* here should be translated "senses."

Colossians 3:16 tells us: "*Let the word of Christ dwell in you richly in all wisdom, teaching and admonishing one another in psalms and hymns and spiritual songs, singing with grace in your hearts to the Lord.*"

This is the very heart of this marvelous teaching. A renewed mind is one where the Word of God dwells richly. That suggests a fullness of fellowship where the heart is the Father's companion through the Word.

Acts 19:20 throws more light on it: "*So the word of the Lord grew mightily and prevailed.*"

It is where the Word gains the ascendancy and rules man's mind through the spirit.

At Ephesus, the Word had gained the ascendancy to the extent that spiritualists "*brought their books together and burned them in the sight of all. And they counted up the value of them, and it totaled fifty thousand pieces of silver*" (Acts 19:19). The Word of God had grown so mightily in that city that it had conquered the works of Satan.

When the Word grows mightily in a church, it brings the people into harmony with the Word. It is the same in an individual.

> But when the kindness and the love of God our Savior toward man appeared, not by works of righteousness which we have done, but according to His mercy He saved us, through the

> *washing of regeneration and renewing of the Holy Spirit.*
>
> *(Titus 3:4–5)*

The Holy Spirit renews our mind and our thinking through the Word. I used to think it would come through prayer, but praying will not renew your mind. You must study, act, or *do* His Word.

The Word is the only thing that will do it. I know men and women who spend hours in prayer, yet there is no renewing of their minds. They are still sense-ruled. Their exposition of the Scripture is childish, immature. The Word has not gained the ascendancy in their minds.

I heard D. L. Moody say just before his death that if he had a chance to live again, instead of spending so much time in prayer, he would spend more time studying the Word.

> *And have put on the new man who is renewed in knowledge according to the image of Him who created him.*
>
> *(Colossians 3:10)*

This means to put on the conduct and the conversation of the new man.

You have just come out of the realm of the old man, the natural man, the fallen man. God has given you new self in place of the old one. You are to *"put on the new man,"* to begin to live the Word, study and practice the Word in your daily life. As your spirit sees it and embraces it, your body responds.

God promised to cooperate with us. His Spirit cooperates with our spirits.

Now you can see the necessity of your taking time to meditate on the Word, to get quiet with the Lord. You had to take time to learn your algebra, your mathematics, your history, and your geography. Now you must take time to sit with His Word and let the Spirit unveil His Word to your spirit.

If you will do it, you will know Him in reality. If you will not do it, you will need to have someone else act for you, pray for you, and believe for you.

God promised to come and associate with your very heart life. I think Paul brings it out most clearly in Galatians 2:20: *"It is no longer I who live, but Christ lives in me."*

It is God who has made His home in my body. It is God who is at work within me. Greater is He who is in me than he that is in the world. (See 1 John 4:4.)

That is where the Holy Spirit has come and identified Himself with you. The Holy Spirit has come to live in your very being. *"Do you not know that your body is the temple of the Holy Spirit?"* (1 Corinthians 6:19). He is there.

I am learning to do this. I become quiet and say, "Blessed Spirit, now make the Word a living thing in my spirit. Open it to me." I go over the passage I want unveiled to me, and I meditate on it. After a bit, the clamor of my mind is gone. The noise it makes is gone.

You can become as noisy in your intellect as you become noisy with your hands and feet.

I grow quiet. Then in a single minute or a half-minute, there will be an unveiling of the Word of God such as I have never seen before.

It does not take Him more than a moment to unveil the Word, to throw upon the screen a message that will take you hours to write. Eternal life has come into your spirit. Now let God have freedom to lead you into the realities of His revelation in the Word.

15

MEN OF THE SENSES VERSUS MEN OF THE SPIRIT

The man who lives in the realm of the senses is unable to understand the things of the spirit.

> *The natural man* [the man ruled by the senses] *does not receive the things of the Spirit of God, for they are foolishness to him; nor can he know them, because they are spiritually discerned.* (1 Corinthians 2:14)

That is why scholasticism frankly denies the authority of the Word and its inspiration.

When we understand that the men who are ruled by the senses cannot know God, see Him, have fellowship with Him, or understand His revelation, we know that their railing against our faith in Christ will have no more effect on us than the babbling of a child.

We do not deny the wonders that have been wrought through the knowledge that comes from the senses. We thank God for them, but we know their limitations. If we call them *men of the body*, we would perhaps understand it more clearly.

If we could once grasp the significance of the fact that all their knowledge has come through their bodies or through some other person's body and that they are of the earth, earthy, we could understand their unbelief. When we realize that Satan governs the body of the *old man*, it will be easy for us to understand how sense knowledge can be colored by Satan without one's being conscious of it.

The men of the spirit are those whose spirits have been recreated. They have received the nature and life of God, and their mental processes have come to be dominated by that life. Their minds have been renewed through the study and practice of the Word.

Let us state once more that the mind of the senses cannot know God. It is enmity against God. It is not subject to the love law of God. It is dominated by Satan's nature.

When the mind of the recreated human spirit gains the ascendancy over the renewed mind of the senses, then God can think through us, speak through us, and make His Word a living thing to us. It becomes God's very Word on our lips.

Some of us have never thought that there were two minds in the believer. There is the sense knowledge mind that has dominated us for so long. Then there is the new mind, the mind of Christ, the mind of the recreated spirit.

Paul prayed, *"That the God of our Lord Jesus Christ, the Father of glory, may give to you the spirit of wisdom and revelation in the knowledge of Him"* (Ephesians 1:17).

You see, God has difficulty in conveying His message through the language of men. The Greek language was the best at the time, but it was inadequate to convey God's thought.

This is what He wants you to understand: Paul was praying that God may give us wisdom in our spirits so that we may understand His revelation that has been given to us. When we understand the revelation or the unveiling of what God wrought in Christ in our redemption, our spirits gain the ascendancy and dominate us.

Notice the next verse: *"The eyes of your understanding being enlightened"* (Ephesians 1:18). Here God is struggling to reveal to us that our heart or recreated spirit can see with God's eyes, hear with God's ears, and think with God's mind that is imparted to us in the Word.

God is faithful, by whom you were called into the fellowship of His Son, Jesus Christ our Lord. (1 Corinthians 1:9)

Fellowship means sharing together. This recreated spirit now shares with Jesus in the knowledge of His redemptive work. It shares with Him the burdens and responsibility of a lost world, the unveiling of Himself through Paul. It shares with Him the Father's life and ability to carry out His will on the earth.

What a thrilling thing it is to know that we are called to share with Jesus in spiritual fellowship. But it does not stop there. Later, Paul says Jesus *"became for us wisdom from God—and righteousness and sanctification and redemption"* (1 Corinthians 1:30).

If He is made wisdom for us, then the very wisdom of God belongs to our spirits. How few mistakes we would ever make if we followed this inward monitor that is so often silenced by the senses and held a prisoner when it should sit upon the throne.

We possess a conscience, which is the voice of our spirits.

You see, Jesus has been made unto us redemption, so our recreated spirits are redeemed from satanic dominion and control. As our spirits gain the ascendancy, our minds become emancipated so that we can think God's thoughts, so we can understand the Word and take advantage of our redemptive rights.

We have God's nature and God's life in us, but it often lies dormant. We have never taken advantage of it. So few have realized the miracle of our being able to partake of the life and nature of God. We are often afraid to let this nature dominate us and have the right-of-way. We hold it in check and let our reasoning faculties dominate us, though they receive all their impulses from the physical body.

Acts 26:16–18 throws more light on this almost unknown subject:

> *I have appeared to you for this purpose, to make you a minister and a witness both of the things which you have seen and of the things which I will yet reveal to you. I will deliver you from the Jewish people, as well as from the Gentiles, to whom I now send you, to open their eyes, in order to turn them from darkness to light, and from the power of Satan to God, that they may receive forgiveness of sins and an inheritance among those who are sanctified by faith in Me.*

This was the Master speaking to Paul. Jesus said that He was going to appoint Paul as a minister and a witness of the things that he had already seen and the things that Christ was to reveal to him.

Notice, now, that he was to open their eyes. In other words, he was to open the eyes of their hearts—not their physical eyes, nor their mental eyes, but their spiritual eyes. This is something that one cannot do for himself. Only God can do it. You remember that He opened the heart of Lydda to receive the message from the lips of Paul. (See Acts 16:14.)

They were to turn from darkness—that is, Satan's dominion and sense knowledge—to the light. They were to turn from Satan to God. They had been walking in darkness under the dominion of the god of darkness. Now they were to come to the revelation light, to the light of life. In other words, Jesus was saying, "He who accepts Me as his Savior and walks in fellowship with Me will have the illumination that only comes from eternal life."

That light is the new kind of wisdom. It is the new kind of love.

The spirit of the one who receives it is no longer under the dominion of Satan. His body doesn't need to be. His mind doesn't need to be. As he walks on with the Lord in the light of life that is given in this revelation, he will take his emancipation from Satan for body and mind. He will be able to say, "He whom the Son sets free is free in reality."

He will then learn to stand fast in the liberty wherewith Christ has made him free.

For you were once darkness, but now you are light in the Lord. Walk as children of light (for the fruit of the Spirit is in all goodness, righteousness, and truth). (Ephesians 5:8–9)

That is a wonderful commentary on "God is light." We are to walk as children of light, children of God.

Ephesians 5:1 says, *"Be imitators of God as dear children."* We are love's children with a love nature, and if we walk in love, we walk in the light. When we stay out of love into selfishness, we are plunged into darkness.

Light here means the wisdom and ability to know where we are going. If we walk in the light as He is in the light—and we can do this—we have fellowship with all the children who are walking in the light and who have intimate contact with our Father.

The Word becomes a living thing on our lips, becomes food and strength for our spirits.

There is a great deal of talk about our getting the proper amount of vitamins in our food. This is an unveiling of divine vitamins.

You walk in love. You walk in the strength of God. You walk in His light and His ability. You walk in fellowship with Him, and you have His strength.

> *Again, a new commandment I write to you, which thing is true in Him and in you, because the darkness is passing away, and the true light is already shining. He who says he is in the light, and hates his brother, is in darkness until now. He who loves his brother abides in the light, and there is no cause for stumbling in him. But he who hates his brother is in darkness and walks in darkness, and does not know where he is going, because the darkness has blinded his eyes.* (1 John 2:8–11)

This new commandment of which John speaks is the commandment given to the new covenant people: *"Love one another; as I have loved you"* (John 13:34).

He said the darkness is passing away, and the true light is shining. Satan's dominion was being broken over men and women, and the light of this revelation of Jesus Christ was dawning in the hearts of the people.

In the old days of darkness, they glorified hatred and the ability to injure one another. Now they glory in their ability to bear one another's burdens, help the weak, and walk in love. They discovered that if a man stepped out of love into darkness, his eyes were blinded. He was filled with confusion and was unable to find his path.

You can see what a large place eternal life and the nature of God holds in the body of Christ.

You have received God's life and nature. That means that you have received a new kind of wisdom, a new kind of love, and a new kind of ability. I like to call it a *lover's ability*, a lover's light on life's problems. It is that kind of ability that gives strength to live as Jesus would in our place.

In reality, we *are* taking Jesus's place. We are bearing the fruit that Jesus would have borne if He were here, except that we are multiplying that fruit by our numbers. Every one of us is a branch laden with this love fruit that helps, heals, saves, and blesses lost men.

The new creation means a new self, a self built out of the love nature of God. It must learn the love language and love habits of this new relationship with Christ.

He tells us to put on the new man, that is, the conduct of the new man. This is taught in the Epistles and the Gospels.

16

I AM WHAT GOD SAYS I AM

To say, "I am what God says I am" is a militant confession. It is declaring war on defeat, failure, and weakness. This is carrying war over into the enemy's tent. This is taking the initiative from the enemy.

> He has delivered us from the power of darkness and conveyed us into the kingdom of the Son of His love, in whom we have redemption through His blood, the forgiveness of sins.
> (Colossians 1:13–14)

This is God talking. He says, "I delivered you out of the authority of Satan. He has no more dominion over you than he has over My Son. I delivered you out of the authority of darkness."

Darkness means uncertainty and lack of assurance. It means halting, hesitant walking; it means that the light has been extinguished, and you are not sure of the next step.

But you have been delivered out of that. You have been translated into the realm of light.

Jesus said, "I am the light of the world. He who follows Me shall not walk in darkness, but have the light of life" (John 8:12).

You have been delivered out of that darkness. Now declare it. Confess it. Repeat right now, "I am delivered out of the authority and dominion of darkness. Satan cannot rule my life because God is the very strength of life, and greater is He who is in me than the demonic forces of darkness."

You dare to make that confession, hold fast to it, and refuse to yield a single moment. You have been delivered *"into the kingdom of the Son of His love,"* in whom you have your redemption. That wipes out everything that you have ever done. It is more than forgiveness. The slate of the past has been wiped clean. You stand complete in Him.

Now in the face of your enemies, you dare to make your confession: "I am what He says I am. If He says I am redeemed, I am. If He says that I am a new creation created in Christ Jesus, I am. If He says that He has translated me into the kingdom of the Son of His love, I am in the love realm under the love law.

"Then as a new creation, I am no longer under Satan's dominion. Jesus is my Lord. Ephesians 2:10 says that I am His workmanship created in Christ Jesus. God has imparted to me His own nature, His own life. I am now a member of Christ's body. This new creation has been born out of the heart of God. I have received God's very nature and life. I am a partaker of the divine nature."

I can hear John whisper in 1 John 5:13: *"These things I have written to you who believe in the name of the Son of God, that you may know that you have eternal life."*

You see, if you have partaken of God's nature, God's life, and the very substance of His being, 2 Corinthians 5:21 is true to you: *"He made Him who knew no sin to be sin for us, that we might become the righteousness of God in Him."*

Notice carefully that as surely as Jesus was made sin for you, you have been made righteous by receiving the life and nature of God. He says you are His righteousness in Christ. You dare to say that you are what He says you are, and you will see that it places you in the realm of victors.

You begin to confess that God has told the truth about you, and you will thrill heaven. You will fill the heart of the Father with joy. You will be repeating John 1:16: *"And of His fullness we have all received, and grace for grace."*

Sense knowledge cannot walk these streets of gold. Sense knowledge cannot get through the gate that leads into the city of fellowship where you are walking with God.

Hear this translation from Weymouth:

> *I pray that Christ may make His home in your hearts through your faith; so that having your roots deep and your foundations strong, in love, you may become mighty to grasp the idea, as it is grasped by all God's people, of the breadth and length, the height and depth—yes, to attain to a knowledge of the knowledge-surpassing love of Christ, so that you may be made complete in accordance with God's own standard of completeness.* (Ephesians 3:17–19 WNT)

Now let us turn to 2 Corinthians 3:4–6:

> *And we have such trust through Christ toward God. Not that we are sufficient of ourselves to think of anything as being from ourselves, but our sufficiency is from God, who also made us sufficient as ministers of the new covenant.*

Here God becomes our sufficiency, our ability. He told the disciples to *"tarry in the city of Jerusalem until you are endued with power from on high"* (Luke 24:49).

The word *power* comes from the Greek word *dunamis*, which means "ability." Jesus said, "I want you to tarry in Jerusalem until you receive God's ability." He is calling that ability "sufficiency" now. He has become your ability, your sufficiency.

Now you can understand Philippians 4:13: "I can do all things in Him who is my ability, my sufficiency, my strength."

You understand that you are taken out of the realm of natural ability, out of the realm of sense knowledge ability, into the supernatural realm of God. God is now not only the strength of your life, but He is your ability.

You can understand 1 John 4:4: "*You are of God, little children, and have overcome them, because He who is in you is greater than he who is in the world.*" This is the surpassing grace of God.

Weymouth's translation is illuminating:

> *For if, through the transgression of the one individual, Death made use of the one individual to seize the sovereignty, all the more shall those who receive God's overflowing grace and gift of righteousness reign as kings in Life through the one individual, Jesus Christ.* (Romans 5:17 WNT)

You have received God's overflowing grace and the gift of righteousness. That enables you to reign as a king in the realm of life through Jesus Christ.

What would that conception of Christianity do for the millions of earnest men and women who are struggling to get faith and get wisdom so that they may walk well pleasing in His sight! They have no knowledge of the Word.

This is a revelation of the grace of God to us who are in the body of Christ. Let us notice further Philippians 4:13 (WNT): "*I have strength for anything.*" God is my ability; He is my wisdom; He is my righteousness; He is my perfect redemption from weakness, fear, and lack. I stand complete in Him, a victor over all my enemies.

Second Corinthians 2:14 is true: "*Thanks be to God who always leads us in triumph in Christ … in every place.*"

He is making Paul a victor, a conqueror, an overcomer; He is enabling the apostle to write this revelation, most of it behind prison bars. Paul was the spiritual conqueror of the ages, and what Paul was in Christ, *you* are in Christ.

Now we can enjoy Isaiah 41:10: *"Fear not, for I am with you; be not dismayed, for I am your God. I will strengthen you, yes, I will help you, I will uphold you with My righteous right hand."*

I want the Spirit to reveal this prophecy and promise that belongs to the church and to the church only. Jesus is God's right hand of righteousness, and He whispers to us, *"Fear not, for I am with you."*

If God is with you, then He is for you. And if He is for you, who can be against you? But what thrills us is this: *"For I am your God."* Think of the Creator of the universe speaking to you like that! This should make you know that you are more than a conqueror.

You see, this is the truth in regard to what we are in Christ when He says, "I will help you, I will uphold you, and I will be your strength and ability." You are not afraid of anything. Fear has lost its dominion. You and Christ are walking in triumph.

If you have eternal life, you have God's nature. If you have God's nature, you have God's righteousness. If you have God's righteousness, you can pray the prayer of the righteous man.

If you have eternal life, you are God's son. If you are His son, you are Satan's master in Jesus's name. If you have eternal life, you are a branch of the Vine. Then you can bear vine fruit, doing the works of God. You are grafted into Christ, and Christ is God.

The vine and the branch are one. The vine is hidden, but the branch is seen, laden with the fruit of love. Men see the vine life in you.

17

WALKING IN THE LIGHT OF LIFE

One of the most illuminating sentences that ever fell from the lips of the Son of Man is in John 8:12: *"I am the light of the world. He who follows Me shall not walk in darkness, but have the light of life."*

This is one of Jesus's many affirmations of what He was. You will remember that He dared to say:

- *"I am the good shepherd"* (John 10:11).
- *"I am the bread of life"* (John 6:35).
- *"I am the way, the truth, and the life"* (John 14:6).

And now He says, *"I am the light of the world."*

First John 1:5 says, *"God is light and in Him is no darkness at all."* God is light. God is the source of light. Now Jesus declares that He is the light of life.

Then we understand this beautiful fact: God is light, and light is love. If one walks in this life, he walks in love, and he walks in the light and the wisdom of the Word. Walking in the light means walking in the Word, acting on the Word. Walking in the light of life means walking in love.

This life is an inner light of the spirit. It is the life of God, and our spirits are radiating love.

Jesus said, "I am the way, the truth, and the life" (John 14:6). The three are all one. The truth is reality, and so Jesus was reality. Jesus was the way into the Father's presence. Jesus is reality in every phase of this divine life.

The Word living in us is God living in us. Living means doing, acting.

THE BELIEVER'S GREATEST DANGER

The believer's greatest danger is to lapse from the light of the Word to the light of the senses. The Gospel of Luke explains this.

> *The lamp of the body is the eye. Therefore, when your eye is good, your whole body also is full of light. But when your eye is bad, your body also is full of darkness. Therefore take heed that the light which is in you is not darkness. If then your whole body is full of light, having no part dark, the whole body will be full of light, as when the bright shining of a lamp gives you light.* (Luke 11:34–36)

You have seen faces illumined with the glory of God upon them. That is the result of eternal life flooding the body and love filling the words. Joy trembles upon the lips. Living and walking in the light of the Word is the most beautiful and thrilling experience known.

To walk in the senses and trust in the wisdom of the senses is dangerous. But one is tempted to do this because everyone around him perhaps lives in the sense realm, and they look upon him as fanatical because he dares walk in the faith realm, the love realm.

You dare practice love when everybody else practices selfishness. You live the Jesus life while they live the self-life. You give, and they criticize your giving. You deny yourself while they live in self-gratification. They cannot understand you.

They didn't understand Jesus. Those most intimate with Him didn't understand. Neither did they understand Paul, Peter, and John in those early days. Then don't expect them to understand you because you live the love life.

You are walking in the light of the Word instead of the light of the senses. The light that is in them is darkness. They are walking in darkness. They know not where they are going, but you walk in the light of love.

There is no occasion of stumbling in you. You act like Jesus; you talk like Jesus. You have the Jesus nature in you, and that Jesus nature is dominating your spirit.

You find joy that is unspeakable and full of glory.

They have found all kinds of trouble, and they are ever advertising their trouble.

You live in the light as He is in the light. Now you can understand what He means when He says: *"I am the light of the world. He who follows Me shall not walk in darkness* [the senses], *but have the light of life"* (John 8:12)—that is, eternal life.

You can't have the light of life without having the love of life, the new kind of love that Jesus brought. You can't walk in love without becoming a seeker after the lost, a burden-bearer of the weak, and a comforter of those in sorrow.

Eternal life is a wonderful thing. It is a solution for all home problems. Yes, it is a solution to the human problem. Men who have eternal life can never take advantage of the weak, but rather, they become their burden-bearers. You will always count it a privilege and a pleasure to deny yourself in order to help someone else.

Jesus becomes big in you.

I can understand now what Paul meant when He said to the Galatian church: "*I am again in travail* [labor pains] *until Christ be formed in you!*" (Galatians 4:19 RSV).

The life of God had not gained the ascendancy in those men who had just left heathenism and embraced Christ as Savior and Lord. Paul yearned over them, longed to help them know their place in Christ.

Christ being formed in us is Christ being built in us through our acting and doing the Word. Life becomes manifest in us as we become "*doers of the word, and not hearers only*" (James 1:22).

A new day has come for the life of God ruling in men, Jesus men with the Jesus nature, the Jesus conduct. The old struggle with sin is past. Man knows what his redemption means, knows that Satan has no dominion over this new creation.

It is not religion; it is the very life of God holding sway in man, this new creation man.

18

ALL THE WORDS OF THIS LIFE

In the midst of the stirring dramatic scenes that surrounded the disciples following Pentecost, there is a little drama that we have overlooked.

The disciples had been arrested for their testimony and for their healing of the man at the beautiful gate.

The Sanhedrin had been incensed because the disciples had proved that they had crucified the Lord of life. They had the disciples locked up, put in a public ward. But at night, an angel of the Lord opened the prison doors, brought them out, and said: *"Go, stand in the temple and speak to the people all the words of this life"* (Acts 5:20).

That sentence has been ringing in my spirit. The Greek word for *life* is *zoe*, which means "eternal life." The angel knew what Jesus had brought to the world. He knew what eternal life meant.

Peter may not have understood it, nor John have grasped it, for the revelation had not yet come to the church through the apostle Paul, but the angel understood and commanded them to proclaim it.

The angel's command thrills us: "*Go, stand in the temple.*" They were to go where all the people were, where the blood of bulls and of goats had been spilled for fifteen hundred years. They were to go where these innocent animals had given their animal life to protect the old covenant people.

Such sacrifice of life was now unnecessary because Christ had made the supreme sacrifice and had brought eternal life. They were to stand in the temple and speak the words of this new kind of life.

The animal's life was given as a covering, as an atonement for the broken law and spiritually dead Israel. But Israel no longer needed the atoning blood of an animal. They were going to receive eternal life into their spirits. They were going to become sons and daughters of God.

The blood of Christ was not a covering. It was to become a recreating power in their spirits. Under the old law, God had said, *"For the life of the flesh is in the blood, and I have given it to you upon the altar to make atonement* [or covering] *for your souls"* (Leviticus 17:11).

Under this new order of grace, He said, "I am giving you eternal life to recreate you, to make you My own sons and daughters. You will no longer need to be covered. Because you are My sons and daughters, you may stand in My presence as though sin had never been."

Now you can understand what the angel meant: "*Go, stand in the temple and speak to the people all the words of this life*" (Acts 5:20).

The new kind of life had come. You and I can understand John 10:10 now: *"I have come that they may have life, and that they may have it more abundantly."*

Jesus brought an abundance of God's nature. They were to become partakers of the divine nature, the very essence and substance of the Deity.

What a difference it would make if ministers would preach eternal life, explaining it to the people instead of preaching sin and judgment! How little they appreciate the fact that sin has been put away, and God is not reckoning unto the world their trespasses. He has committed to us the Word of reconciliation, the Word that gives eternal life, righteousness, and sonship.

Eternal life unites our spirits with Him. His nature comes into our spirits, and we become like Him. This gives us faith in ourselves. We have been failures in our own sight. Now we are linked up with God, with success. Days of failure are past. We have come into our own.

19

THE NEW MAN

We have learned that the dominant forces in the universe are spiritual. They manifest themselves physically. It has been hard for us to realize that man, the real man, is a spirit and manifests himself through his physical body.

The body is a temporal home in which man lives, but man is in the class with God.

We have never realized clearly that disease and sickness head up in our spirits. The mind is not cognizant of them until the body is affected and the senses have communicated the fact to the brain. Back behind all of this, however, is that disease had fastened itself upon the spirit before it was communicated to the body.

It took me a long time to see this, but as I dealt with sick folks, I found that as I opened the Word to them, their spirits accepted the Word, their minds endorsed it, and instantly, their bodies were delivered.

Then I could see that diseases were spiritual things, and I could understand Isaiah 53:4–5 (YLT):

Surely our sicknesses he hath borne, And our pains—he hath carried them, And we—we have esteemed him plagued, Smitten of God, and afflicted. And he is pierced for our transgressions, Bruised for our iniquities, The chastisement of our peace [is] on him, And by his bruise [or His stripes] there is healing to us.

When we speak of cancer, it is a physical thing. But our diseases are all spiritual just as our sins are spiritual, and they were laid upon Jesus.

SIN IS A SPIRITUAL THING

Sin may manifest itself in a physical act, but behind the physical act is the spirit that directed it. All that was laid on Jesus.

When physical disease manifests itself in the believer's body, the believer knows that the disease was borne by Jesus. He knows that disease has been put upon him by the adversary, so he rebels against the adversary's putting the disease on him that Jesus has borne. He commands it to leave him in the name of Jesus. The disease has to go because it is there by the will of the adversary.

The believer says, "Demon, in Jesus's name, leave my body." And when the demon leaves, he takes the disease with him.

Someone says, "Mr. Kenyon, that isn't sense."

I know. We are not dealing with sense knowledge. We are dealing with spiritual realities. These spiritual things are just as real as sense things.

Or do you not know that your body is the temple of the Holy Spirit who is in you, whom you have from God, and you are not your own? For you were bought at a price; therefore glorify God in your body and in your spirit, which are God's.

(1 Corinthians 6:19–20)

You remember in Philippians 1:20 that God is magnified in our bodies, glorified in our bodies, for Paul writes, *"So now also Christ will be magnified in my body."*

These bodies of ours cannot glorify Him, nor magnify Him, when they are full of disease. But when they are clean and shine with the presence of the Spirit, the Father is glorified. If the church takes her place, there will no longer be any sickness in it.

Today sickness runs rampant in the church.

We know that disease cannot lay its hand upon us when we recognize that we have God in us, that it is God who is at work within us, willing and working His own good pleasure. (See Philippians 2:13.)

We are immune to colds and fevers. No disease can fasten itself upon us or our loved ones because in Jesus's name, we have *"all authority"* over them. (See Matthew 28:18.) We are clothed with God's ability.

GOD'S ABILITY

Jesus told His disciples to *"tarry in the city of Jerusalem until you are endued with power from on high"* (Luke 24:49). That means to be clothed with God's ability. This is ability to deal with disease, demons, and circumstances. Isn't it thrilling that we common men and women have such uncommon ability from God?

I want you to notice another remarkable thing:

> *Therefore, if anyone is in Christ, he is a new creation; old things have passed away; behold, all things have become new. Now all things are of God, who has reconciled us to Himself.*
>
> (2 Corinthians 5:17–18)

We are a new species, a God-created species. God's life has performed a miracle. God's love nature has been imparted to us. It has driven out the old nature. The old things have passed away.

The old self has been displaced by a new self, born of God. The old things of hatred, jealousy, bitterness, cursing, and all the other vile habits that we have cultivated have passed away. New habits are being formed in this new creation.

The life of God is gaining the ascendancy where spiritual death held sway. God's nature, which is love, is displacing the unpleasant traits of the old nature.

We love where we once hated. We reign as kings where we once served as slaves.

Wonderful, isn't it? Clothed with God's ability, we live a dominant victorious life in Christ.

HIS WORKMANSHIP

"*For we are His workmanship, created in Christ Jesus*" (Ephesians 2:10). See what you are—His workmanship! He did it. So *"put on the new man which was created according to God, in true righteousness and holiness"* (Ephesians 4:24).

He built us out of righteousness, out of His very heart, out of His very being. We are born of God.

Can you see how we are equipped by a new nature to meet the great spiritual forces that are destroying the human race, how we are equipped not only to conquer the demonic forces but to bring joy, hope, life, and victory to the sin-ruled heart?

Can't you see that we are not left to our own ability, but we have in us the very life and ability of God? Can't you see that this new creation is a love affair, and that we are going to live and walk in love?

THE NEW LAW OF LOVE

Jesus said, "*A new commandment I give to you, that you love one another; as I have loved you, that you also love one another*" (John 13:34).

This new commandment is the new law of the new creation, the men with eternal life. It is the love law of the new covenant. We are going to live and walk in love.

We have lived and walked in selfishness; now we are going to love. We will no longer fight. We will no longer argue and struggle to have our own way, but we who are strong are going to bear the infirmities of the weak and not please ourselves.

This new man with the love nature takes no account of evil. (See 1 Corinthians 13:5.)

This new love life makes us just like Jesus. Jesus and the Father are one. We are going to be one with them.

This new type of Christianity is the greatest thing in the world. It is the righteousness of God imparted to man by God, giving to him His own nature, eternal life. This new type of Christianity is based upon the Word.

THE GREAT CONFESSION

Christianity is called the great confession. Hebrews 4:14 says, "*Seeing then that we have a great High Priest who has passed through the heavens, Jesus the Son of God, let us hold fast our confession.*"

And we read in Hebrews 3:1, "*Therefore, holy brethren, partakers of the heavenly calling, consider the Apostle and High Priest of our confession, Christ Jesus.*"

What do these verses mean by *confession*? It is not a confession of sin, but a confession of our faith in the redemptive work that God wrought in Christ.

It is a fact that faith is dependent upon our confession. If we have a hesitant, faltering confession, our faith will be weak and ineffectual. When we boldly confess the integrity of the Word, faith keeps pace with our confession. Jesus is the High Priest of this great confession.

If you never confess your righteousness, it will be of no value to you. If you never confess His indwelling presence, He will never manifest Himself in your life.

Few of us have appreciated the relationship of a good confession to righteousness. Just as soon as you begin to acknowledge that you are the righteousness of God in Christ, sin consciousness begins to lose its dominion over you and the fullness of the revelation of God in Christ becomes a reality to you.

Faith shrinks at a confession of sin consciousness and shrivels under it.

Faith grows and becomes robust under the confession of our righteousness in Christ. The two grow strong and vigorous by confession. We must confess what we are in Christ. We must confess what He is to us, what He is in us, and what we are in Him. This threefold confession builds us up in the Word. It also builds the Word into us.

It is the Word on our lips that builds faith into others, that awakens them to the study of the Word, that drives them to give up the things of the senses and trust in the reality of the Spirit.

Every time you confess that by His stripes, you are healed, no matter what the senses register with regard to your body, your faith grows.

One just came to me and said, "How can I confess before my neighbors while I have this difficulty?"

I said, "That is your difficulty. You have lowered your confession to meet the demands of the senses rather than declaring that what God has said is. When you denied that Word, the disease gained the ascendancy and faith lost its place."

Change your confession, and you will challenge the reality of the Word. It will become to you what it says that it is.

This new nature feeds on the Word; it must express itself. It will not gain the ascendancy over your reasoning faculties unless you give it freedom through your confession. God wishes to speak through you.

One goes to the level of his confession. Your confession binds you, imprisons you to its level.

God can be no bigger in you than you confess Him to be.

Disease is conquered by our confession.

20

THE FATHER-GOD CONSCIOUSNESS

He was just God to us, and He was a theological God at that. Most of our young preachers in the early days when I began my ministry were theological preachers. They had cold philosophy from Germany, which had gained the mastery over our theological institutions. They gave us a theological Christ, a theological Spirit, a theological Bible, and a theological God.

No one ever called Him *Father* in those days. No one knew Him as Father except here and there, where someone had been led by the Spirit into the love life of the Father.

One day, John 17:23 came to me: "*That the world may know that You have sent Me, and have loved them as You have loved Me.*"

It seemed as though a person had suddenly come out of the bosom of the Father and come down to my level and enwrapped me in a consciousness that I had never dared to believe. At first, I held back and said, "No, it can't be true."

But the music was so entrancing, it drew me against my will. I kept whispering. "No, it can't be true. He can't love me as He loved Jesus. I know how unlovely I am. I know how unworthy I am."

Then He came nearer to me. He drew me to Himself. I heard a voice whisper to me softly, "What business have you to say that you are unclean after I have cleansed you? What right have you to declare yourself unrighteous after I have made you righteous? How dare you voice judgment on the new creation that I have created in My Son?"

I could not keep the tears back. I said, "Forgive me, Lord. Forgive me, Father. I knew not what I was saying. I have been held in the bondage of sense knowledge for so long that I cannot think in terms of spiritual truth. And when You say that You love me, even as You loved Jesus, it seems just a little more than my heart can grasp."

I felt my heart growing warm under the thrill and wonder of His love until I dared to whisper, "The Father loves me; yes, loves me, cares for me, watches over me, feels a personal interest in me, and is ambitious for my success in life." When I saw it, I whispered softly, "My Father, my own dear, wonderful Father, my Father-God."

I had never said it with this new consciousness.

Now I said, "Father, I love You. I love You, Lord Jesus. I love You, great Holy Spirit, You who have led me into this truth. I love this Word that You have inspired. I love this lonely walk with You if You will hold me by the hand."

He is my Father.

Now I know what Jesus meant when He said, *"My Father, who has given them to Me, is greater than all"* (John 10:29).

He is no longer God to me. He may be God to my neighbors, but to me, He is my Father, my own Father. He had been my

Father God ever since I received eternal life, but I did not know it. I did not know I had eternal life until I had been a Bible teacher for years.

I knew that I had my sins pardoned. I knew that I had been justified. I had been converted, but knew nothing about eternal life, the nature of God, that was in me.

How it thrilled me when I knew I had eternal life.

I had received eternal life but didn't know it. He was my Father, and I didn't know it. I didn't know Him in reality. Christianity was a religion to me that was made up of marvelous experiences. Now it became a holy family affair, a relationship. I was God's very own child. He became my very own Father. Oh, the thrill and wonder of it!

Now I could say, "Good night, Father" as I closed my eyes in slumber. In the morning, I could whisper, "Good morning, Father dear. I've another beautiful day to walk with You."

Life was changed. Christianity was no longer a religion but a family affair, a holy, wonderful family affair.

21

CULTIVATING OUR OWN SPIRITS

The knowledge of the effect of eternal life on man's spirit is yet in its infancy.

Man is in God's class of being. He is a spirit, made in the image and likeness of God. When he fell, his spirit became estranged, separated from God.

The human heart has never been satisfied with anything that the world could give. The heart hunger, the spirit hunger of man, is perhaps the most outstanding feature of man's life.

We have learned how to cultivate our bodies and develop them to become athletes. We have learned how to cultivate the intellect, so we have become mental gymnasts. We have found that there is almost no limit to the development of the human mind.

But there has never been a teacher or a chair in any university to teach us how to develop our spirits.

Your spirit is the real you. It is the part of you that contacts God, the part of you that is recreated and receives eternal life. It is the part of you that should dominate your thinking faculties. It is the part of you that gives personality or color to you.

We speak of men with courage. It took me a long time to realize that courage is not a product of the thinking faculties, that faith and love are not products of the thinking faculties.

Faith, love, courage, hope, and fear are not the products of your intellect. You cannot reason fear out of your spirit any more than you can reason love into it.

The thing that differentiates us from each other is, in reality, our human spirits.

Love is not the product of the intellect. You cannot reason love into people. I have tried that. It cannot be done.

The Word was given to us by the Holy Spirit. It was given to us to fit and develop our spirit natures. It is a remarkable thing that when a man is born again, his mind is not touched. His mind needs to be renewed and brought into fellowship with his spirit after he is born again.

> *And do not be conformed to this world* [or age], *but be transformed* [or transfigured] *by the renewing of your mind, that you may prove what is that good and acceptable and perfect will of God.* (Romans 12:2)

You cannot know the Father's will or walk in His will unless your mind is renewed. You will not enjoy fellowship and communion with Him until that time comes. You will not enjoy the riches of His grace until your mind is renewed.

His Spirit, through the Word, has recreated you. You were born again through the Word. It is the Spirit that operates through the Word.

God makes contact through that Word with our spirits and begins to build His life and nature into us. That makes us new creations. Then that nature begins to dominate us through the Word. Only as the Word dominates us do we develop.

The great majority of men and women are failures in life. Success only comes through your spirit gaining the dominance over your intellect. I was amazed when I saw this.

Wisdom is the paramount need of man. It is spiritual.

You may have all kinds of knowledge; you may have all that our universities can give you, all that travel, reading, and experience can give you, but that knowledge is of very little commercial value unless you have wisdom to use what you have.

I know men and women who have very limited knowledge but have much wisdom and because of that, they make a success of life where the man with a great deal of knowledge is a failure.

Wisdom does not come from the intellect. It cannot be given to you by any teacher. The schools cannot make you wise. They can give you a vast amount of knowledge if you are willing to study, but they cannot give you the ability to use that knowledge.

Wisdom is a thing of your spirit. Until your spirit gains the ascendancy in you and dominates your mind, you will never have a great deal of wisdom.

THE VALUE OF RIGHT MEDITATION

The most deeply spiritual men and women I know are people who have given much time to meditation. You cannot develop spiritual wisdom without meditation. God told Joshua this fact at the very beginning of his ministry after the death of Moses:

> *This Book of the Law shall not depart from your mouth, but you shall meditate in it day and night, that you may observe to do according to all that is written in it. For then you will make your way prosperous, and then you will have good success.*
>
> *(Joshua 1:8)*

In other words, God was telling Joshua that meditating on His laws would enable him to deal wisely in the things of life.

Take time to meditate in the Word. Shut yourself in alone with your own spirit where the clamor of the world is shut out. If you are ambitious to do something worthwhile, I would suggest that you take ten or fifteen minutes daily for meditation. Learn to do it. Begin the development of your own spirit.

Perhaps you have gone to school or are going to school for the development of your intellect. Perhaps you are taking physical culture for the development of your muscles.

If you take the time, you can develop your memory.

A man told me of one the other day who had developed his memory until, riding from Seattle to Chicago, he could remember the license of every car that he made an attempt to remember. He could not only remember things like that, but he could remember everything else collected with the trip.

An Indian friend told us one night that there was a time when the Indian could commit to memory the entire New Testament. He would sit and listen to the white man read it through three or four times and he had it committed to memory.

Memory is of the spirit.

You may develop any gift that you wish, but the most important gifts that God has given to you are the spiritual gifts. It is the development of this spirit that is going to mean more to your life than any other thing.

Let me show you some tremendous facts in connection with the development of your spirit life.

When Jesus went away, He promised to send the Holy Spirit.

And I will pray the Father, and He will give you another Helper, that He may abide with you forever—the Spirit of

> *truth, whom the world cannot receive, because it neither sees Him nor knows Him; but you know Him, for He dwells with you and will be in you.* (John 14:16–17)

There is coming, Jesus said, a Spirit that is going to recreate your spirit. Then He is going to take charge of your spirit and dominate you spiritually. You are going to yield your spirit to the domination of the Holy Spirit through the Word.

The psychologist told us that we had a subconscious mind, but it was the spirit, the real man.

The next problem was how my spirit could be developed. Jesus said the Holy Spirit would come and guide us into all reality—not the reality of the intellect, but into the reality of spiritual things.

That is why I want you to get quiet a little while. I want you so quiet that the Holy Spirit may communicate with your spirit through the Word and unveil these truths to you. It will make you a master.

The great body of men do not meditate in the spirit. They live in the realm of the senses. Their meditations are guided by the senses.

The sense-governed mind is limited, but your spirit has practically no limitations. You can develop your spirit life until you dominate circumstances. Your spirit can come into vital union with His Spirit, the Father Himself.

Your spirit becomes a partaker of the divine nature. It is not your intellect or your body, but your spirit that fellowships the riches of His gracious presence. Your spirit, with God's nature in it, can fellowship on terms of absolute equality with God Himself.

Do you see your limitless possibilities?

Someone came to me the other day and said, "In your little book on healing, you say that diseases are spiritual." It is true, but they could not grasp it. They thought that diseases were either mental or physical.

Christian Science says disease is mental. So Mary Baker Eddy became the most outstanding mental healer that the world had ever known.

Jesus brings us into contact with spiritual things, not mental ones. Spiritual things are as real as physical things. They are as real as mental things. Your spirit can reach the point where the things in His Word will become as real to you as Jesus is real to you, as any loved one is real to you.

That can be true. Hear what He said in John 16:13:

However, when He, the Spirit of truth, has come, He will guide you into all truth; for He will not speak on His own authority, but whatever He hears He will speak; and He will tell you things to come.

The Holy Spirit is to take the things of Jesus and the things of the Father and unveil them to us.

The other day, I sat by a sick one who had a cancer. I got her mind off the disease and her physical body, and I began to unfold the Word to her as quietly as I could. I held her down to that Word because I knew the Word could heal her.

When I went into the room, she was filled with fear; she thought she had to have that cancer cut out at once or death would come.

I began to deal with her spirit. I did not tell her so. I did not tell her that healing was spiritual. I did not tell her that the cancer was spiritual and had been manifested in her physical body. I made her see that back yonder, God laid that cancer on Jesus. It was laid upon His Spirit. His Spirit became cancerous with her cancer and the cancers of the world.

He was made sin; He was made sick.

This woman saw that her cancer was laid on Him just as others have. She lay there, and after a bit, she said, "The pain is gone. I am healed."

The Word healed her spirit. That healed her mind and her body.

We have never given the Word its place in our thinking.

The Word is God speaking. The Word takes Jesus's place in life today. The Word living in us means that it functions in us, acts in us, rules in us. We do the Word.

22

DEVELOPING THE HUMAN SPIRIT

In Galatians 5:22, Paul speaks of the fruit of the recreated spirit: *"But the fruit of the Spirit is love, joy, peace, longsuffering, kindness, goodness, faithfulness."*

That is not the fruit of the Holy Spirit. He doesn't bear fruit. We are the fruit-bearing part. We are the branches of the vine. The recreated human spirit linked up with Christ, grafted into the vine, is the fruit bearer.

I have never desired anything more than I have to know how to develop the recreated human spirit.

I believe I have some suggestions that will teach us how to obtain love, how to appropriate it in Christ, how to make it our own. This will teach us how to walk in love so that our conduct will be Jesus-like.

If we could learn how to walk in love and make it the business of our lives, we would solve many problems of human relationships that we thought were impossible.

Jesus lived in love. He lived in the realm of love. He spoke love. His words were love-filled. His acts and deeds grew out of love. He could not help healing the sick; love drove Him. He could not help feeding the multitudes; love compelled Him.

If we could have our spirits developed in love like that, we could live like the Master. We could maintain a real, a beautiful fellowship with the Father, with the Word, and with one another.

In John 14:16–17, Jesus promised that He would send the Holy Spirit:

> *And I will pray the Father, and He will give you another Helper [or Comforter], that He may abide with you forever—the Spirit of truth, whom the world cannot receive, because it neither sees Him nor knows Him; but you know Him, for He dwells with you and will be in you.*

This Comforter He calls *"the Spirit of truth."* He is to guide us into all truth or reality. He is to take the things of Jesus and of the Father and unveil them to us. That is what our hearts are craving.

He is not going to guide us into sense knowledge but into revelation knowledge. He is going to take those wonderful truths in the Pauline revelation and make them a reality to us. In order to do this, it will be necessary for us to have quiet hours, a little while each day set apart for meditation.

Under the new covenant, we are to let the Word of Christ dwell in us richly. We are to abide in the Word, and the Word is to abide in us. This will lead us into the prayer life, into prayer conquests.

Here is another suggestion:

> *Be anxious for nothing, but in everything by prayer and supplication, with thanksgiving, let your requests be made known to God; and the peace of God, which surpasses all understanding,*

will guard your hearts and minds through Christ Jesus.
(Philippians 4:6–7)

In nothing are we to allow anxiety to govern us, *"but in everything by prayer and supplication, with thanksgiving,"* make our requests known to the Father. Then we are to leave them there. When we do that, the Father declares that His peace will come in like a garrison of soldiers into a turbulent country and quiet us.

Then He tells us the things that we are to think about. Read it over carefully:

> *Finally, brethren, whatever things are true, whatever things are noble, whatever things are just, whatever things are pure, whatever things are lovely, whatever things are of good report, if there is any virtue and if there is anything praiseworthy— meditate on these things.* (Philippians 4:8)

We cannot feed on scandal, on nonsense, or on stories that are unseemly and expect to develop in grace. The Spirit will not help us do that.

There must be times when we can sit quietly with the Lord and the Word and meditate upon it until the Word absorbs us and we absorb the Word, until the Word is being built into our mental processes as well as into our spirit lives, until it absolutely governs our thinking.

Do you see what that implies? The renewing of our minds is absolutely necessary. The average believer's mind is not renewed.

> *I beseech you therefore, brethren, by the mercies of God, that you present your bodies a living sacrifice, holy, acceptable to God, which is your reasonable service. And do not be conformed to this world, but be transformed by the renewing of your mind, that you may prove what is that good and acceptable and perfect will of God.* (Romans 12:1–2)

That transformation takes place by the renewing of our minds. How does that come about? By meditation in the Word. By practicing the Word and letting the Word rule us.

> *And have put on the new man who is renewed in knowledge according to the image of Him who created him.*
> (Colossians 3:10)

Our minds are renewed after the image of Him who created us. This means that the Jesus image is going to be reproduced in us until after a while, it will be no more we who live, but Christ living in us—*"Until Christ be formed in you!"* (Galatians 4:19 RSV).

It is possible to build the very Jesus life into us with the Word. The Word never becomes a part of our lives until we act it. It is living this Word, having it live in us in our daily life, that counts.

Share your heart life with Him, as you would with a lover, a roommate, a husband, or a wife, until you exclaim, *"It is no longer I who live, but Christ lives in me"* (Galatians 2:20). Share with Him until the vine life becomes your life.

Become *"filled with all the fullness of God"* (Ephesians 3:19). God's fullness takes us over, dominates us. His fullness of love, His fullness of grace, His fullness of wisdom, healing, and ability displace all the weaknesses and failures that exist in our lives.

Jesus has come on the scene to take over the business. He does it according to His ability that is at work within us.

We must learn to become God-inside minded, to cultivate a consciousness of His indwelling presence, the presence of the living One in us. Remember John saying, *"You are of God, little children"* (1 John 4:4). That is our source. That is our genealogy. That is our comfort and faith builder.

Israel had long pages of genealogy dating back to Abraham, but our chronology is brief. We are *"of God,"* and *"He who is in you is greater than he who is in the world"* (1 John 4:4). The God inside is greater than any difficulty or problem outside. We have been fortified within. Here is the source of real strength. It can become a reality to us if we meditate upon it.

Sometimes as I have sat meditating, it seems as though I could become absolute master of everything, as though there were no longer any impossibilities. *"All things are possible to him who believes"* (Mark 9:23). This becomes a thrilling reality to my spirit.

RIGHTEOUSNESS CONSCIOUS

Of all the truths that the Father has unveiled to us, it seems to me that there is none that equals the consciousness of our righteousness.

The church has preached sin, weakness, and failure for so long that we have become conscious of our failure, our weakness, and unworthiness. We have struggled for faith. We have tried to believe, and all our struggles have been futile. We have found ourselves weaker than when we first began, and we wondered what the reason was.

It was because we did not know that we have been made *"the righteousness of God"* in Christ (2 Corinthians 5:21). The Father looks upon us as though sin had never touched us. He sees His own nature in us. He sees us *in the beloved*.

When my heart saw this, my reason refused to acknowledge it. I said, "No, that cannot be. I could not be like that. It is contrary to all my experiences." Sense knowledge could not register it. It had no way to understand it.

I went back to the Word again and saw it: *"He made Him who knew no sin to be sin for us, that we might become the righteousness of God in Him"* (2 Corinthians 5:21). By the new birth, He had made me His righteousness.

I surrendered to that Word. I yielded to it. I no longer questioned or argued. I said, "What God says, is. If He has made me a new creation, if He has made me out of true righteousness and holiness, I must be what He says I am though I have never been taught it and have never understood it." I stood in the presence of His declarative statement that I am what He says I am.

How my heart leaped for joy! I could not stay in the house. I walked the streets. My whole being was singing a new anthem of praise and worship and love.

God says that I am His righteousness, that I am without condemnation. He has called me into fellowship with His Son. He Himself has crowned my life with joy. It was all His work. I did not have to do anything but accept it.

I wasn't passive. No, I was aggressive. I said, "Father, if that is what belongs to me, I am taking it now and thanking you." I became conscious of my righteousness, conscious that He is mine and that I am His, that all He said in the Word, He has made good. I rest with joy in the consciousness of this newfound source of victory.

Then it began to unveil itself to me. I said, "If I am the righteousness of God, then I can go into His throne room without fear. I can stand in His presence without any sense of weakness or failure. He has invited me to come *"boldly to the throne of grace"* (Hebrews 4:16).

I was no longer afraid of disease. I was no longer afraid of old age. I was no longer afraid of physical infirmities. I was no longer afraid of the lack of money.

In order to practice love, I gave up all I had and have since been giving it up. I am poor and yet I am so rich with His presence, so joyful with the consciousness that my Father is watching over me, caring for me.

I know that I have a right to the use of Jesus's name. I know that I can cast out demons in His name, for He said, "*In My name they will cast out demons ... they will lay hands on the sick, and they will recover*" (Mark 16:17–18). I have become a master.

The lordship of Jesus is not only over me, but it is also in me and through me. He is not only my Lord, but He is also the Lord over disease when His name is on my lips. As He conquered want and hunger, storms and tempests with the Father's words in His lips, so now He is going to conquer things with the Father's own Word on my lips.

How it thrills! Now we see the wonder of eternal life, the miracle of it. I will let this life loose in me. The wonder of His grace, that He has given me His own nature. I am one with Him; as the branch is to the vine, so am I to Him.

The days of weakness are past. The new day of grace is real.

He is to me what He says He is. I am to Him what He says I am. This is the realm of life, the place where the sons of God abound in grace and joy.

I am His child. His home is my home.

23

SPIRITUAL GROWTH

The Word calls the real man—the spirit man, the part of us that is recreated and can know God and fellowship with Him—*"the hidden man of the heart"* (1 Peter 3:4 YLT).

He is the hidden man to sense knowledge. The modern psychologist has never found him. They have given him a new name: *the subconscious mind.* They have discovered that he is there, but they do not know who he is or what his functions are.

In Romans 7:22, he is called *"the inward man."*

The outward man is the visible, seen man as spoken of in 2 Corinthians 4:16: "Even though our outward man is perishing, yet the inward man [or spirit] *is being renewed day by day."*

You understand that this inward man is an eternal man. He doesn't know time or age. He is always fresh and new.

The body, the home of the senses, grows old and feeble. Senses fail to function, but the spirit is always young.

In Ephesians 3:16, Paul prays that the Father "*would grant you, according to the riches of His glory, to be strengthened with might through His Spirit in the inner man."* Here is the secret of a rich spiritual understanding of the Word, an intimate fellowship with the Father, and a growing faith.

You understand that faith and love are the fruits of this recreated human spirit. This recreated inner man, this hidden man of the heart, is the part of us that can become intimate with the Father. It is he that grows in grace and in spiritual discernment of revelation knowledge.

The church has never studied this phase of man.

The psychologist, who has only natural human reasoning, can never know this inward man. It can be safely said that the psychologist can never know himself unless he has eternal life, for only the man who is recreated can know himself. Only revelation knowledge can show us our true selves. This new man can't know himself unless God unveils the truth through the Word.

You can understand now why textbooks on psychology cannot survive a decade. They are all theories of sense knowledge.

Here is revelation knowledge and the Word of truth to aid the psychologist to know himself.

The psychologist and the philosopher are God-hungry spirits searching for reality. The only place they can search is in the realm of the five senses, their own human body. They have talked much about functional psychology. They have learned much by observing the effect of each one of the senses on the mind.

Sense knowledge is limited to knowledge that we gain from the senses. It is limited to the physical world.

When a man finds Jesus Christ, he has no further need for sense-ruled philosophy or psychology, for he has found the thing his spirit has craved: reality. Jesus is reality.

The real man is *"the hidden man of the heart"* (1 Peter 3:4 YLT). The *inward man* that is being renewed day by day is the real man, the spirit man. This inward man is granted strength and ability through the Holy Spirit according to the riches of the Father's glory. (See Ephesians 3:16.)

This strength and ability is given so that Christ in the Word may dwell in that recreated spirit to the end that he is *"rooted and grounded in love"* (Ephesians 3:17). He can then grasp the fullness of his redemption, the reality of his righteousness, and the sense of mastery over his enemies.

Your human spirit is united with the Deity, as the Deity was united with humanity in Christ. Now your spirit can grasp John 15:5: *"I am the vine, you are the branches."*

The vine is a divine Person; the branches are divine persons.

God was incarnate in the flesh in the Person of Christ. We are incarnate in the spirit in Christ. We are *"partakers of the divine nature"* (2 Peter 1:4). We are actual members of the body of Christ. Our spirits are joined with one another so that the body becomes one.

A NEW PSYCHOLOGY

Our spirits are joined with Christ, so Christ and the individual spirit become united in a holy oneness.

Man was created in the same class with God, as an eternal spirit in the image and likeness of its Creator. Before man sinned, he had perfect fellowship with God. He lived in the realm of the spirit. But when he committed high treason and was driven from the presence of God, he became dependent upon his senses for his protection and life.

His spirit became the slave of his senses.

However, for many generations, you can see the spirit's influence upon the mind. This is seen in the architecture before and after the flood. They have uncovered five cities built one upon another in

Mesopotamia. The last one to be discovered, which was evidently built before the flood, shows the finest type of architecture.

Anthropology proves that no matter how far we go back in Egyptian and Babylonian history, we still find a form of relatively high civilization. There is no record of a Stone Age in either land. After a while, however, the spirit was overshadowed, the senses gained the supremacy, and man lost all real knowledge of spiritual things.

Senses absolutely controlled man at the time of the first covenant with Abraham. Abraham was evidently the only one of his age who had any spiritual discernment, unless, as tradition tells us, Shem was still alive and was Abraham's teacher. Shem believed God's Word in the face of the testimony of his senses. Abraham's faith is the true type of the faith of the believer today.

When Jesus came, all men lived in the realm of senses. If you carefully read the four Gospels, you'll notice that they had only sense knowledge faith. They believed what they could see, hear, taste, and feel. Their spirits had no place in their daily life.

Until the believer recognizes the two kinds of faith—one based on sense knowledge and the other based on the Word of God—he'll never be able to enjoy his privileges in Christ.

You remember Thomas is the outstanding exponent of sense knowledge faith. After the resurrection, before he had met Jesus, he said to those who had seen the Risen One, "I will not believe until I can put my finger into the wounds of His hands and my hand into His side." (See (John 20:25.) Some days later, Jesus appeared again, and this time, Thomas was there.

> Then He said to Thomas, "Reach your finger here, and look at My hands; and reach your hand here, and put it into My side. Do not be unbelieving, but believing." And Thomas answered and said to Him, "My Lord and my God!" Jesus said to him, "Thomas, because you have seen Me, you have believed.

Blessed are those who have not seen and yet have believed."
(John 20:27–29)

Can't you hear the pathos in Jesus's voice when He speaks to Thomas?

Oh, it is so hard for the sense knowledge folks to believe. They are struggling, praying, and crying for faith everywhere, but faith doesn't come that way. Faith comes by getting acquainted with the Father through the Word. It does not come by studying the Word alone, but by actually living the Word, doing the Word, practicing the Word, and letting the Word live in you.

The multitude said, "Show us a sign that we may believe." Jesus said, *"An evil and adulterous generation seeks after a sign"* (Matthew 12:39).

That generation didn't seek a sign any more than our generation does. Let any man be advertised to speak who has spectacular manifestations and he will fill the house. Why? Because this generation does not believe the Word. It believes in signs and wonders, something that the senses can register. The Jews lived in the realm of the senses.

On the day of Pentecost, a new era began. We call it the dispensation of the Holy Spirit. That is only half of the truth. It is the dispensation of the recreated human spirit. The cultivation of our spirits comes through our giving our spirits right of way in our daily walk; it comes by listening to the spirit and letting it rule our reason.

You remember Jesus quotes from Deuteronomy: *"Man shall not live by bread alone, but by every word that proceeds from the mouth of God"* (Matthew 4:4; cf. Deuteronomy 8:3). God's Word is inspired by the Holy Spirit and is the food for the recreated spirit.

As we meditate in the Word and become doers of the Word, our spirits slowly but surely gain the ascendancy over our sense-ruled minds.

You remember in Romans 6:12, the Spirit says, "*Do not let sin reign in your mortal body, that you should obey it in its lusts.*"

Sin reigns in the senses. There is nothing wrong with the physical body. The wrong is in the senses gaining control of our minds and causing us to do the things that we should not do. Our spirits are brought into subjection to the senses when members of the body that are governed by the senses gain control.

Your conscience is the voice of your recreated spirit. As the spirit is educated in the Word, the conscience or the spirit's voice becomes more and more authoritative.

I have come to believe that if one fellowships with the Word under the illumination of the Holy Spirit, after a bit, our human spirits can become perfect guides. What we have called a *hunch* is simply our spirits speaking to us.

I have found that women in the home have discernment of spirit more readily than do men. In the business world, the professional world, and the daily work in factories and shops, sense knowledge dominates. The homemaker receives more and more of the mind of the spirit as she meditates in the Word and fellowships with the Father.

> *To set the mind on the flesh* [the senses] *is death* [ruled by spiritual death], *but to set the mind on the Spirit is life and peace. For the mind that is set on the flesh is hostile to God.*
> (Romans 8:6–7 RSV)

The mind of the spirit can fellowship with God. The Word is the food and life of the recreated spirit. If we walk in love, the spirit has perfect freedom to guide us. You can understand that faith and love both come from the recreated human spirit. Faith grows as we practice love. And as we practice love, the Father becomes more and more real to us. The Word becomes more and more precious. Its hidden secrets are revealed to us.

First Corinthians 2:12 declares, "*Now we have received, not the spirit of the world* [ruled by the senses], *but the Spirit who is from God, that we might know the things that have been freely given to us by God.*"

Our spirits that have received their life from God are able to know the things of God, while the natural mind, dominated by the senses, is unable to know the things that are freely given to us in the redemptive work of Christ. The natural man can't understand the expression *in Christ* or what it means, but the God-taught recreated spirit grasps it with eager joy.

We can see now that the greatest need of the present day for the church is the renewing of the minds of the believers and the education and development of the recreated spirit.

As Paul describes in 1 Corinthians 3:1, "*I, brethren, could not speak to you as to spiritual people but as to carnal, as to babes in Christ.*"

The word *carnal* here means "sense ruled." They are mere babes. They walk according to sense knowledge "*in the manner of men*" (1 Corinthians 15:32). They are full of jealousy, bitterness, and selfishness. They have never learned the way of love. They are full of talk, but they are not doers of the Word.

24

THE LORDSHIP OF JESUS

In the early days, when I first saw the teaching of His lordship, I was a bit fearful of Him. I used to say, "If I should recognize His lordship over my life, I would fear that He would lead me to do things I would not care to do and to go places where I would not care to go."

I did not know then that His lordship was the lordship of love. I did not know that my happiness and my joy depended on His governing my life. I did not know that independence on my part spelled misery and mistakes. I did not know that I could do all things in Him. I did not know that He could make me a master of circumstances.

I saw the truth in Philippians 4:11: *"I have learned in whatever state I am, to be content."* But I did not know what it meant. In a large measure, I had interpreted the Word with sense knowledge.

Now I stopped interpreting it, and I began to practice it. I began to *do* the Word as James tells us. (See James 1:22.) As I practiced the Word, there came an unveiling of the Master such as I had never seen before. His very heart seemed to be uncovered.

I came to know Him with a spiritual intimacy that I had never realized possible.

It was not until then that I understood Psalm 23:1–3:

> *The Lord is my shepherd; I shall not want. He makes me to lie down in green pastures; He leads me beside the still waters. He restores my soul.*

I saw that my soul was my reasoning faculty, and that He restored it into fellowship with my recreated spirit.

I had been drunk with desire for success. I had been drunk with sorrow. I had been drunk with unbelief and fear.

Now He restores my soul, my mind, so that it is in perfect fellowship with the Word. My mind agrees to live love. I had not agreed to love before; I had not realized that the Father was love, His will was love, and His way was the love way. I had never agreed to this love program. Now I see it and understand it. I joyfully agree to it.

THE LORDSHIP OF LOVE

The lordship of Jesus is really the lordship of love. The recognition of the lordship of love puts us over into the very position that Jesus occupied in His earth walk. He recognized the lordship of the Father's love over His life.

You can feel it as you read the Gospel of John. The Spirit lifts the curtain in that gospel and lets us look upon Jesus and the Father in sweet fellowship. We see Jesus living love, acting love. He is living His Father's Word just as we are to live the Word. He is living love, as we are to act love. What a lordship this is!

"*The Lord is my shepherd; I shall not want*" (Psalm 23:1) takes us out of the realm of fear and want. It carries us over into the green pastures. The alfalfa is growing knee-deep. There are plenty of shade trees. Everything is beautiful. The hillsides are covered with flowers, and birds are singing in the trees.

We revel in the joy, love, and fellowship that our hearts have craved. It enwraps us now and holds us almost spellbound in this newfound lordship of love. We cannot know or appreciate this new kind of love until we receive eternal life. Receiving eternal life brings us into the realm of love.

We know that this life is the nature of the Father, and the Father is love. So as we yield ourselves to Him, He pours that life abundantly into us. Life becomes big, with joy filling our hearts to overflowing.

We are in His will. We are where He can use us, call us when He needs us. We are in the inner circle, as John and Peter were in Christ's earth walk. He depends on us. We become His messengers, ambassadors of love. What a life this lordship gives!

Come, walk this love-lighted way, this Father-pleasing way.

25

THE GREAT SPIRITUAL FORCES IN THE WORLD

Few of us realize that the greatest forces are not material, but spiritual. The things that dominate men are not dollars, bonds, or lands but the spiritual forces that drive men after these.

There are two major destructive forces in the world, coming from Satan: hate and unbelief. From God comes two major constructive forces: love and faith. These great spiritual forces are dominating the human race now. Man's will must choose between God's will and Satan's.

There never was such a need for clear, intelligent teaching about love and faith as there is today. Every university should have a course in these two major forces that govern the human race. Men must be taught to believe if they are going to win.

Hate and unbelief have caused all the insurrections in morals, finances, economics, and nations down through the ages.

Few people know the destructive power of unbelief or the constructive, creative power of faith.

Hate and unbelief come from the same source. They never produced a great soul, a great nation, or a great enterprise. They destroy every nation where they have gained the ascendancy. They are the enemy of prosperity and peace. Some time ago in Russia, the head of the educational board declared that love and faith, as taught in the New Testament, are the enemies of communism.

Love and faith are of God. God has been the constructive force in all the ages. Love and faith have produced the highest civilization, the finest characters, and the greatest enterprises.

God is love. He acts and speaks by faith. He is the Author of all peace, plenty, happy homes, hope, faith, and love.

Satan is the author of hatred. He acts in the realm of unbelief. He is the author and source of poverty, sickness, broken homes, the drink traffic, the dissensions, and hatred that dominate the human race.

It is most important that we recognize the place that Jesus gave to faith in His three years' public ministry. We hear Him say, *"If you have faith like a mustard-seed ... nothing shall be impossible to you"* (Matthew 17:20 WNT)

"All things are possible to him who believes" (Mark 9:23). Faith unites man with the omnipotence of God.

Jesus said, *"I am the vine, you are the branches"* (John 15:5). Jesus was God's faith manifested.

First John 4:7–8 gives us the definition of faith with a statement regarding it: *"Beloved, let us love one another, for love is of God; and everyone who loves is born of God and knows God. He who does not love does not know God, for God is love."*

There's a new definition of real Christianity, of the new creation. Everyone who loves is born again and knows God. He who does not love does not know God.

Love gives birth to faith. Here is the statement of faith: *"For God is love."* Christianity is defined as a love life, a life dominated and ruled by love. The kind of love mentioned here is the new kind of love that Jesus brought to the world.

There are two kinds of love in the world. The Greek words for them are *phileo* and *agapa*. *Phileo* is human love, the best thing that natural man has outside of Christ. It is a failure. The other kind of love is the nature of God manifested in the new creation.

The human love is the goddess of the divorce courts. The new kind of love has never been known to go to a divorce court. The new kind of love that Jesus brought would be the solution of the family problem and the home problem; it gives real faith in the family.

The great fact is that God Himself is love. He is the love God. This makes Him the real faith God.

THE FAITH GOD

Hebrews 11:3 tells us that this love God is also a faith God. This fact is new to most of us. We have become used to the thought that God is love, but we have never thought of Him as the faith God.

"Now faith is the substance of things hoped for, the evidence of things not seen" (Hebrews 11:1). In other words, faith gives reality and substance to the thing that we had only wished for, hoped for. Hope is always future. Faith is now.

We hope for Christ's return. We hope for heaven. It is our heavenly hope, our messianic hope. But hope is not faith. He who believes has; believing is possessive. Hope is always future. Faith has given substance or reality to the thing that we had longed for and hoped for, but had no evidence that we would ever get.

It is a conviction of the things not seen. It is actually thanking God for money that has not yet come. It is thanking God for healing that has not been manifested, but that we are as sure of as if it were manifested.

Faith gives substance to the things that we wanted. It gives reality to things that have never been seen. We have not seen the money, but we know it is here.

Hebrews 11:3 goes on to say, *"By faith we understand that the worlds were framed by the word of God, so that the things which are seen were not made of things which are visible."*

This staggers reason. Here is the declarative statement that the worlds, the stellar heavens, have been created by the Word of God; they were not made out of anything that is seen. They are a distinct and positive creation. They came into being by the Word of God.

> *Then God said, "Let there be lights in the firmament of the heavens to divide the day from the night; and let them be for signs and seasons, and for days and years; and let them be for lights in the firmament of the heavens to give light on the earth"; and it was so. Then God made two great lights: the greater light to rule the day [the sun], and the lesser light [the moon] to rule the night. He made the stars also.*
>
> (Genesis 1:14–16)

God spoke the whole universe into being. Man says that it is not credible. Sense knowledge cannot grasp it. It is above sense knowledge. All that sense knowledge can do is guess. Hypothesis after hypothesis have been exploited and exploded.

Here is a Being great enough to speak a universe into being and govern it. That Person is our Father God. This is creative faith.

CREATIVE FAITH

Every great financial institution has been the product of some man's faith.

The great chemical industries that represent the greatest financial institutions in the world are products of faith.

Frank W. Woolworth said, "Let there be," and a sixty-million-dollar enterprise came slowly into being.

Andrew Carnegie said, "Let there be," and the great steel industries began to take form.

Man is a faith creation. By faith, God created him. Man never reaches his highest development through unbelief. Doubt gives birth to fear, and fear has never produced a great character. The world's great characters have been the products of faith. They have been molded in faith. Faith has been the mighty force that has driven them on to produce the miracles of civilization.

Abraham believed God. His body and Sarah's were renewed after he was one hundred years old, and she was ninety years old. They gave to the world a son, Isaac. Abraham stands as a signpost on the road to mighty achievements by faith.

Matthew 14:13–21 is the story of Jesus feeding the five thousand with five loaves and two fish. That was creative faith. Jesus spoke and that food multiplied.

Faith has been creative wherever it has had an opportunity to exercise itself. Faith is creative today. You dare to begin to bless the human race, with that little handful of meal and that little cruse of oil, and you will see it multiply in your hands. Elijah was an example of creative faith. (See 1 Kings 17:12–16.)

Jesus healing the lepers, restoring clean flesh where it had been destroyed by that deadly disease, was an example of creative faith.

Today in the mechanical world, the mechanical inventions are brought into being by creative faith. It is creative faith where the chemists are struggling to bring forth something they have dreamed was hidden in metal, coal, and in the vegetable world. They dreamed. Then they began to create in their spirit natures. This creative faculty is not in man's mind, but it is in his spirit, behind his mind.

The great poet does not reason out his poetry. His reason tells him if the meter is correct, or if he has used the right words. But the dream came from his spirit.

It is the spirit that produces faith. Man's spirit is the channel through which love pours itself upon the human race. Love and faith are not the product of reason. They belong to the higher self in man.

DOMINATING FAITH

In Moses, we see a picture of faith dominating the laws of nature. Israel was just freed from the bondage of Egypt, but the Egyptians were following after them. Moses's people were confronted with an impassable wilderness on the one hand and the Red Sea on the other. Moses began to cry out to God.

> And the LORD said to Moses, "Why do you cry to Me? Tell the children of Israel to go forward. But lift up your rod, and stretch out your hand over the sea and divide it. And the children of Israel shall go on dry ground through the midst of the sea." (Exodus 14:15–16)

It was faith speaking to the Red Sea. It was faith that lifted up the rod. See the result. The sea opened. That slimy, muddy bottom of the sea suddenly became firm, dry ground with grass growing like a park as the psalmist tells us.

Faith made a way where reason stood helpless. Faith opened a path in the sea and congealed the waters in that hot climate. They looked up on either side of them and saw the waters frozen solid, holding back that mighty force that would have engulfed them. Faith ruled the laws of nature.

The three Hebrew children thrown into the fiery furnace give us an illustration of faith dominating heat. The laws of nature were absolutely obedient to the faith of those young men. (See Daniel 3:19–27.)

It was faith that calmed the Sea of Galilee while the disciples cowered in fear.

> *Suddenly a great tempest arose on the sea, so that the boat was covered with the waves. But He was asleep. Then His disciples came to Him and awoke Him, saying, "Lord, save us! We are perishing!" But He said to them, "Why are you fearful, O you of little faith?" Then He arose and rebuked the winds and the sea, and there was a great calm. So the men marveled, saying, "Who can this be, that even the winds and the sea obey Him?"* (Matthew 8:24–27)

Here Jesus is tenderly chiding them because of their fearfulness.

Matthew 14 relates the story of Jesus walking on the waves at night in the midst of a storm. The disciples are filled with fear, but He says, "Be of good cheer! It is I; do not be afraid" (verse 27).

> *And Peter answered Him and said, "Lord, if it is You, command me to come to You on the water." So He said, "Come." And when Peter had come down out of the boat, he walked on the water to go to Jesus. But when he saw that the wind was boisterous, he was afraid; and beginning to sink he cried out, saying, "Lord, save me!" And immediately Jesus stretched out His hand and caught him, and said to him, "O you of little faith, why did you doubt?"* (Matthew 14:28–31)

It is a challenge for the church to walk by faith, but this is what God wants. He wants us to walk in the realm of the miraculous. That is simply living in the realm of the spirit.

The non-miraculous life is lived in the realm of the senses. Spiritual things are just as real as physical things. God wants us to dominate the laws and forces of nature.

The destructive laws of nature came into being when man fell, and Satan gained the ascendancy over the earth. Jesus came to restore man's lost dominion. He came to restore joy and plenty, to destroy poverty, pain, and want. Faith today could destroy poverty, disease, sickness, and want of every kind. Faith today could bring peace and quietness back to the human race.

But unbelief has gained the ascendancy, and unbelief causes moral, spiritual, and mental storms. They cause the awful destruction by war, waste, and selfishness. Jesus is saying to the church, "Oh, ye of little faith. Why can't you come and walk with Me? Why can't you dominate the unhealthy and the unhappy surroundings of life?"

Can't you hear Him say, "I can do all things in Him who strengthens me?" (See Philippians 4:13.) The ability of God is in me. It is not I but Christ who dwells in me. "It is God who is at work within you, willing and working his own good pleasure." (See Philippians 2:13.)

If you would let God loose, you would dominate circumstances just as Jesus dominated them. Instead of being ruled by the petty bitterness of the world around you, you rise in triumph over it.

The winds and waves obeyed Jesus. The winds of bitterness and hatred will obey your faith.

God created the world with words. Jesus multiplied that bread and fish with words. Jesus hushed the sea by saying, *"Peace, be still!"* (Mark 4:39). And the winds and the waves obeyed.

Can you see the connection? He says, "Hold fast to your confession." (See Hebrews 4:14.) Your confession is made up of words. *"They overcame him* [the adversary] ... *by the word of their testimony"* (Revelation 12:11)—that is, their confession.

We are to dominate demons with words. In Acts 16:18, Paul said to the demon in the girl, *"I command you in the name of Jesus Christ to come out of her."* The demon came out. Words caused it.

Peter said to the man at the gate of the temple, *"Rise up and walk"* (Acts 3:6). It was the words that caused the man to walk.

Jesus said to the man lying at the pool of Bethesda, *"Rise, take up your bed and walk"* (John 5:8). Jesus healed the man with words.

He has given you words. Words are as potent as they ever were. You say to that woman who has been sick for years, "In the name of Jesus Christ of Nazareth, rise and walk."

There are hundreds in our fellowship who came to us with incurable diseases. They are now going about perfectly well. What did it? It is the dominating power of faith-filled words.

Can't you see what love-filled words have done? Love-filled words have given us marriage, home, and heaven. The mother who rules her home with love-filled words has a happy home.

The mother who rules her home with hate-filled words has a hell to live in.

The man who attempts to rule men with hate and selfish words will only awaken the selfishness and meanness in the men he tries to dominate. But faith, working through love, will fill the hearts of men with joy, victory, and success.

When will we learn the tremendous power of words filled with faith?

HEALING FAITH

Matthew 9:20–22 has a beautiful illustration of healing faith:

Suddenly, a woman who had a flow of blood for twelve years came from behind and touched the hem of His garment. For she said to herself, "If only I may touch His garment, I shall be made well." But Jesus turned around, and when He saw her He said, "Be of good cheer, daughter; your faith has made you well." And the woman was made well from that hour.

The Greek word used here is *sozo*, which means "heal." That woman had healing faith, faith that would not be denied. She had heard what Jesus had done for others. She evidently knew many had been healed. Now she said within herself, "If I but touch him, I am healed."

Jesus's words consummated the healing of this woman's body. It was the word of the Master that healed almost everyone.

Men are healed today by words. I have laid my hands upon thousands and said, "In the name of Jesus Christ, by His stripes, you are healed." The diseases have left their bodies. They have been instantly healed. Cancers, tumors, ulcers, arthritis, and numerous other incurable diseases have responded to the word of faith that we preach.

Psalm 107:20 says, *"He sent His word and healed them."*

It is the healing word, the word of faith that does the work. This Bible is the word of faith. This Bible on your lips becomes the healing Word. These written pages have no power to heal, but when they are translated into your life and become a part of you, you utter them with lips of love and Satan's power is broken and diseases are healed. Men and women arise with joy.

Acts 27:20–44 is the story of Paul's shipwreck. He dared to stand before that company of sailors and passengers and say, "An angel of God stood by me last night and told me that we are going to go onto an island, and that every soul is going to be saved."

They could not believe it. For fourteen days, they had suffered agony, not having seen the sun. That vessel had been driven and buffeted by the sea. Paul said, *"I urge you to take nourishment, for this is for your survival, since not a hair will fall from the head of any of you"* (Acts 27:34). Then he blessed the bread, and they ate.

Faith gripped that crew of men. They acted on the Word. Paul's faith in the Word of God dominated the situation. Every soul was saved from a watery grave.

Philippians 1:28 (WNT) is a remarkable statement in regard to faith:

> *Never for a moment quail before your antagonists. Your fearlessness will be to them a sure token of impending destruction, but to you it will be a sure token of your salvation—a token coming from God.*

It is your putting up a solid front before the world. It is your daring to act on the Word in the face of every evidence of failure. You know that God cannot lie, and He watches over His Word to perform it. You dare to act on the Word.

You may know all of these blessed, mighty promises. You may understand all the great teachings of the Word, but they are of no value to you until you act on them.

It is the Word that you act upon that brings results. Believing is acting. *"He who believes has eternal life"* (John 6:47 RSV). That is to say, he who acts upon the Word of God has eternal life. He is healed.

He who acts upon the Word of God is saved. He who acts upon the Word of God cannot be put to shame.

Romans 10:9–11 is the challenge of grace to the broken, wrecked hearts today:

> *If you confess with your mouth the Lord Jesus and believe in your heart that God has raised Him from the dead, you will be saved. For with the heart one believes unto righteousness, and with the mouth confession is made unto salvation. For the*

Scripture says, "Whoever believes on Him will not be put to shame."

This is God's eternal Word. Do you want faith? Faith comes by acting on the Word of God. Romans 10:17, *"Faith comes by hearing, and hearing by the word of God."* Hearing means acting, doing the Word of God. You will never have faith until you act on the Word of God.

You may have mental assent, and you may glory in the Word and tell how beautiful it is. That is fine, but it does no good. You must act on the Word. Step out of the realm of failures into the realm of success. Become a dominator of circumstances rather than a slave to the conditions around you.

Be creative as Jesus was and as men down through the ages have been who dared to act upon the Word of God and see what God will do for you.

Paul knew that he possessed eternal life, the nature of God. He gloried in it. He was not ashamed to confess it. He said, *"I am not ashamed, for I know whom I have believed and am persuaded that He is able to keep what I have committed to Him"* (2 Timothy 1:12). Paul knew what he had. Paul rejoiced in his confessions.

Second Corinthians 2:14 is his song of triumph, faith's mighty victory: *"Now thanks be to God who always leads us in triumph in Christ, and through us diffuses the fragrance of His knowledge in every place."*

Triumphant faith that cannot be conquered, that will not yield no matter what the appearances may be, knows God cannot lie and *"Whoever believes on Him will not be put to shame"* (Romans 10:11).

This makes us act like sons of God. We use the name of Jesus against the forces that oppose us. We are masters, united with omnipotence.

26

THE REALITY OF THE WORD

The Father has magnified His Word by calling His Son the Word.

> *In the beginning was the Word, and the Word was with God, and the Word was God.* (John 1:1)

> *And the Word became flesh and dwelt among us.* (John 1:14)

That is the eternal *logos*, the Word. The Father has glorified the Word, this written Word that becomes a living Word when filled with faith on our lips. It becomes a life-giving Word. It becomes a healing Word. It becomes an educational Word in the things of the Spirit.

It is the Word that the Spirit uses to unveil the things of Jesus to us. It is the Word that He uses when He unveils the things of the Father to us.

> *And take the helmet of salvation, and the sword of the Spirit, which is the word of God.* (Ephesians 6:17)

I wondered if that word *spirit* there meant the recreated human spirit. The Holy Spirit cannot use the Word except as He uses it through our lips. The Word is only used through the lips of the recreated.

We are going to think of it now as the sword on the lips of the recreated man or woman. It is the Word filled with love that melts hearts. It is the Word filled with truth that cuts men to the very quick and makes them cry out in agony.

It is the sword of the recreated spirit. It is not only a sword, but it is also the *balm of Gilead*. (See Jeremiah 8:22.) It is the healing, gentle, tender words of the Father. It has in it the hushing, quieting spirit of love that is in a mother's heart when a child is wounded.

What a wonderful thing it is to live in the reality of the Word, to have the Word on our lips filled with the energy of God—blessing, saving, and recreating men and women, healing the sick, and breaking the power of demons over men's lives. What a thing it is, this living Word!

We hold in our hands the written Word. When we become filled with the Spirit and love gains the mastery, it becomes a living Word on our lips; it becomes a prevailing Word over the forces of evil around us. It prevails over doubt and fear. It prevails over ignorance, failure, and weakness in men.

Acts 19:20 tells us, *"So the word of the Lord grew mightily and prevailed."*

How our hearts thrill with the consciousness of having the very *logos* of God on our lips, knowing we can fill this Word with love and grace and pour it out upon men and women. The miracles recorded in the book of Acts were all performed by the Word of God. Jesus, the *logos*, was in the Word on the lips of the apostles.

The multitudes of men and women who have been healed, saved, and built up in Christ during my ministry have been blessed through the living Word on human lips.

Those who have eternal life can use this life-giving Word to bless men. The Word becomes a living thing on the lips of those who have eternal life; otherwise, it is a dead thing.

When we let God loose in us, His Word has life and healing in it; our lips become the medium through which He pours eternal life into men. The Word is God speaking. It is a part of Himself. The Word and God are one in blessing men.

The Word of God created the universe. The Word has creative ability today on your lips. Dare to let it work through you.

The Word can't fail you. It is God speaking through your lips. Give it freedom. It is God's faith Word. He believes in His Word. He knows His Word will not return unto Him void. Act on it, love it, and do it.

27

WHAT WE ARE IN CHRIST

I was surprised to find that the expressions "in Christ," "in whom," and "in Him" occur more than 130 times in the New Testament. This is the heart of the revelation of redemption given to Paul.

Here is the secret of faith that conquers, faith that moves mountains. Here is the secret of the Spirit's guiding us into all reality.

The heart craves intimacy with the Lord Jesus and with the Father. This craving can now be satisfied.

Ephesians 1:7 says, "*In Him we have redemption through His blood, the forgiveness of sins, according to the riches of His grace.*" It is not a beggarly redemption, but a real liberty in Christ that we have now. It is a redemption by the God who could say, "*Let there be lights in the firmament of the heavens*" (Genesis 1:14) and cause the whole starry heavens to leap into being in a single instant.

It is omnipotence beyond human reason.

This is where philosophy has never left a footprint.

Our redemption is a miracle of His grace. It is according to "*the riches of His grace.*" It is a present-tense work wrought "*through*

His blood." It is lavish. It is abundant. Our redemption is a perfect thing. When you know it, enter into it, and your heart grows accustomed to it, there will be ability in your life that you have never known.

You are delivered out of the authority of Satan. You are free. It is in Him that you have your redemption. You have been delivered out of Satan's dominion. You have been conveyed *"into the kingdom of the Son of His love"* (Colossians 1:13). You are free from the dominion of Satan.

The hour will come when you awaken to the fact that he cannot put disease upon you, that he cannot give you pain and anguish in your body. The hour will come when you will know that want and poverty are things of the past as far as you are concerned.

You will understand Psalm 23 is for you, and you will shout amid the turbulence and fear of other men, "The Lord is my shepherd. I do not want. He makes me lie down in plenty, in fullness. I am satisfied with Him."

This redemption is real. Satan is defeated, disease is outlawed, and want is banished. We are free. John 8:36 says, *"Therefore if the Son makes you free, you shall be free indeed."* Robert Young's translation (YLT) says, *"If then the son may make you free, in reality ye shall be free."*

In John 10:10, Jesus says, *"I have come that they may have life, and that they may have it more abundantly."* What is life? Life is the nature of God. You may have the Father's nature abundantly. You are *in Christ*, in the Father's presence. You are in the very realm of life.

This realm of life has in it the life that transcends reason. We have eternal life, God's very substance.

In John 14:6, Jesus says, *"I am the way, the truth, and the life."* The truth is reality. He was unveiling His heart to us, showing what He can be to us in our daily life. He can be all that His heart of love desires to be to those whom He has redeemed.

He can be reality to us. How our hearts have craved this! He can fulfill every desire of our hearts.

Paul says, *"Stand fast therefore in the liberty by which Christ has made us free, and do not be entangled again with a yoke of bondage"* (Galatians 5:1). The gravest danger to the believer is the possibility of his lapsing back into bondage after he has been made free. He leaves the realm of the spirit and faith and walks in the realm of the senses. As sense reason gains the supremacy, he loses his joy in the Lord.

Therefore, if anyone is in Christ, he is a new creation.
(2 Corinthians 5:17)

We are new creations in Christ Jesus. We are just finding out what this can mean to us. This new creation fact gives you all that it means to Jesus and the Father whether you know it or not.

Paul's revelation is filled with new creation truth. It is God's dream for you to enjoy the fullness of this new creation's privileges.

"Old things have passed away" (2 Corinthians 5:17). Those old things of bondage, fear, doubt, want, sickness, weakness, and failure are gone. You say, "That is not possible." But it is. The new creation is just like the Master. He is its head.

Jesus says, *"I am the true vine, and My Father is the vinedresser"* (John 15:1) and *"I am the vine, you are the branches"* (verse 5). He is the vine; you are the branch. As He is, so are you.

As long as you deal in doubts and fears, as long as you sit in judgment on yourself, you will never arrive. You will never enjoy these things. If, however, you will act on the Word—act on it as you would act on news from a friend—you will arrive. When you read, *"All things have become new"* (2 Corinthians 5:17), start thinking of yourself as living in this new realm.

You have been reconciled to God through Jesus Christ. You have perfect fellowship with Him now. Oh, the wealth that belongs to you in this new relationship! Dare to act your part.

Ephesians 2:10 says, *"For we are His workmanship, created in Christ Jesus."* If you are His workmanship, you are satisfactory to Him. He is pleased with you.

We have preached condemnation and sin for so long that we do not know how to preach righteousness and tell the people what they are in Christ. When someone does tell them, they feel that it is false teaching. They feel that anything is false teaching that does not honor sin and lift it into the place of Christ.

You are God's new man. His Word declares that He brought the new man into being:

> *Having abolished in His flesh the enmity, that is, the law of commandments contained in ordinances, so as to create in Himself one new man from the two, thus making peace.*
> (Ephesians 2:15)

The new man *"was created according to God, in true righteousness and holiness"* (Ephesians 4:24). The new creation knows but one Lord. Jesus is the Lord of the new creation.

Colossians 2:6–7 gives us a graphic statement of facts:

> *As you therefore have received Christ Jesus the Lord, so walk in Him, rooted and built up in Him and established in the faith, as you have been taught, abounding in it with thanksgiving.*

What a glorious truth! No longer are you a weakling. His strength is your strength. We are so strong that we are to abound in thanksgiving. When we stop abounding in thanksgiving, we deteriorate spiritually.

> *The Lord is my light and my salvation; whom shall I fear? The Lord is the strength of my life; of whom shall I be afraid?*
> (Psalm 27:1)

The Lord is your shepherd; you shall not want. (See Psalm 23:1.) You swing free from the old prison house of bondage, fear, and want, of hunger and cold. You are out in the freedom of God.

Hebrews 7:25 is Jesus's present attitude toward you: *"Therefore He is also able to save to the uttermost those who come to God through Him, since He always lives to make intercession for them."* Seated at the Father's right hand, He ever lives to make intercession for you. Say it aloud, "He ever lives for me." Just as the wife lives for the man she loves, so in a greater measure the Lord Jesus lives for you. He has only one business: that of living for you.

WE ARE HIS RIGHTEOUSNESS

Of all the wealth that is known to the human heart, there is nothing that equals this: Jesus declares through the apostle Paul that we are His righteousness.

I cannot grasp it. We are His righteousness. How precious we must be to Him!

He once became our righteousness. He once declared us righteous by His resurrection from the dead. Now He goes beyond the declaration and makes that a reality.

> *He made Him who knew no sin to be sin for us, that we might become the righteousness of God in Him.*
> (2 Corinthians 5:21)

We have become *"the righteousness of God in Him."* Yet there is more:

> *But of Him you are in Christ Jesus, who became for us wisdom from God—and righteousness and sanctification and redemption.* (1 Corinthians 1:30)

Note these three blessed facts:

1. God becomes our righteousness. (Romans 3:26)
2. Jesus is made righteous for us. (1 Corinthians 1:30)
3. And we have become the righteousness of God in Him. (2 Corinthians 5:21)

> *The life which I now live in the flesh I live by faith in the Son of God, who loved me and gave Himself for me.*
>
> (Galatians 2:20)

He loved me. He gave Himself up for me. What love is revealed here! He not only redeemed me and sanctified me, but now before heaven, He says, "I am that man's redemption. I am that man's sanctification." Then I can hear His voice rise to notes of utter triumph when He shouts, "I am his righteousness and his wisdom."

This is all His work. It is not man's works lest he should say, "I had a share in that." Your repenting, crying, and weeping had naught to do with your righteousness or your redemption. You stand complete in Him, in all the fullness of His great, matchless life.

Romans 8:33–34 is the climax of the revelation of our redemption:

> *Who shall bring a charge against God's elect? It is God who justifies. Who is he who condemns? It is Christ who died, and furthermore is also risen, who is even at the right hand of God, who also makes intercession for us.*

You are God's elect. Jesus and the Father have elected you, and now He says, "Who shall lay anything to the charge of My own son or My daughter?" There is only one person of any standing before the Supreme Court who could lay anything to your charge. That is Jesus—and He will not do it.

Can't you see the wealth of your position? Can't you see the riches of the glory of your inheritance in Christ? You are in Him. All that He planned in Jesus is a heart reality now.

There is no condemnation for you. There is no judgment for you. There is no fear of death for you. Why? Because death is simply swinging the portals open for you to march in triumph into the presence of your Father.

First John 4:18 grips the heart: *"There is no fear in love; but perfect love casts out fear."*

In Christ, we have received eternal life, the nature of our Father. That nature is love. That love is perfect. Our human love is imperfect. His love is *agape*, the love that makes life beautiful. You may not perfectly understand or perfectly enter into it, but it is His perfect love, and it is all yours now.

> *For as the body is one and has many members, but all the members of that one body, being many, are one body, so also is Christ.* (1 Corinthians 12:12)

We are so one with Him that we are called Christ. The church is called the Christ ones, Christians.

He is the vine; you are the branch. *"He who abides in Me, and I in him, bears much fruit"* (John 15:5). As the branch is to the vine, so are you to the heart of Jesus. You are utterly one with Him.

All this time, you have been thinking about your sin, your weakness, and your failings. Hear Him whisper to your heart now from Romans 8:1: *"There is therefore now no condemnation to those who are in Christ Jesus."*

If you are born again, you are *"in Christ."* You are a conqueror. You are free from condemnation. You are the righteousness of God in Him. You are the fullness of God in Him. You are complete in Him.

The wealth of His glory, the wealth of His riches, have never been sounded. You are righteous. There is no sin consciousness for you. There is no inferiority complex for you. You are now in Christ, the very righteousness of God. You can use the name of Jesus without fear.

You can do as Peter did in Acts 3:5–6: "*So he gave them his attention, expecting to receive something from them. Then Peter said, 'Silver and gold I do not have, but what I do have I give you: In the name of Jesus Christ of Nazareth, rise up and walk.'*"

You can swing freely.

Whatever you ask the Father in Jesus's name, He will give it to you. (See John 16:23.) John 15:7 is yours now: "*If you abide in Me, and My words abide in you, you will ask what you desire, and it shall be done for you.*"

You are in Him. He is in you. His Word abides in you. You are His righteousness. You are His life. You can do His works now.

> *He who believes in Me, the works that I do he will do also; and greater works than these he will do, because I go to My Father. And whatever you ask in My name, that I will do, that the Father may be glorified in the Son.* (John 14:12–13)

You take your place. You use Jesus's name to heal the sick. His death was not in vain. His suffering was not in vain. You stand complete in His completeness, filled with His fullness. You are filled with His holiness. His grace is yours.

Hebrews 4:14 can become a reality in you: "*Seeing then that we have a great High Priest who has passed through the heavens, Jesus the Son of God, let us hold fast our confession.*"

The word here is not *profession* but *confession*. Christianity is called the *great confession*. Your confession is what you are in Christ. All that we have said to you is a reality. You hold fast to it.

The adversary will try to make you deny your confession. He will try to make you confess anything rather than this. He will try to make you confess weakness, failure, and want. But you hold fast to your confession: "My God does supply every need of mine." (See Philippians 4:19.) You stand by that confession.

You say with Paul, "*I can do all things through Christ who strengthens me*" (Philippians 4:13). You make the declaration that He is the strength of your life. Say it aloud to yourself until you get accustomed to hearing it.

First Peter 2:24 says this of Jesus: "*Who Himself bore our sins in His own body on the tree, that we, having died to sins, might live for righteousness—by whose stripes you were healed.*" You died unto sins with Christ on that cross, you arose to walk in righteousness, and by His stripes, you are healed.

When Jesus arose from the dead, healing belonged to you. Hold fast to your confession in the face of every assault of the enemy. Rebuke it in the name of Jesus.

You walk in the way of righteousness, which means acting and living as though the Word was spoken to you by Jesus. That is the way of victory. That is the way where you cast out demons and disease in the name of Jesus.

Every disease that has afflicted a Christian could have been healed if there had been anyone who had dared to walk in righteousness for that believer, who would have dared to walk in the fullness of his privileges in Christ. The devil could have been driven out and healing could have been his.

> *For we do not have a High Priest who cannot sympathize with our weaknesses, but was in all points tempted as we are, yet without sin. Let us therefore come boldly to the throne of grace.* (Hebrews 4:15–16)

You are invited to come now to the throne room and sit with the Master and with the Father. You are to come boldly. Don't come creeping in. Don't come in confessing your sin, bewailing your weakness and failures. Put on the new garment. Dress fittingly to appear before the throne.

You are the sons and daughters of God Almighty, without condemnation. You will find mercy and grace to help in time of need.

28

SOME MIGHTY FACTS

There are some things eternal life has given us. If we realized what we were in Christ and knew that we had the ability to be what God says we are, our lives would be transformed in a week.

We do not understand what redemption and the new creation have made us. We do not realize what we are to the Father's heart and what He is to us. Most of us are theological Christians instead of Bible Christians. We have theological experiences and are ever attempting to square the Word with those experiences.

We have been taught there is no truth beyond our creed. We lock our people in a creed, making them prisoners of the theories of men born a hundred years ago. The creed Christian is not a Bible Christian. Each creed must have a Bible translated to fit it.

We have discovered a Christ who is greater than the creeds, a redemption that is greater than the creeds, a new birth that bursts the bonds of creedal Christianity and sets the prisoners free.

We are discovering a type of Christianity that is better than the creeds, better than anything to which the creeds have given birth. The creeds, beautiful though they may be, are largely born of sense knowledge.

Through the redemption that is in Christ Jesus, whom God set forth as a propitiation by His blood, through faith, to demonstrate His righteousness. (Romans 3:24–25)

Our redemption, our Redeemer, is Christ. No one can rob you of your redemption. If you take Christ as your Savior, He becomes your redemption. You become independent of man. Your redemption was God's own work, and He Himself is satisfied with what He did in Christ.

Ephesians 2:10 says, *"For we are His workmanship, created in Christ Jesus for good works, which God prepared beforehand that we should walk in them."* And *"In Him we have redemption through His blood, the forgiveness of sins"* (Ephesians 1:7).

If you have your redemption, you are redeemed. Your redemption was through the blood of Jesus Christ. You have the remission of your trespasses.

Notice first you have your redemption in Christ. It is through the blood of the Son of God. You have remission from all that you ever did before you became a Christian. This redemption is according to the riches of His grace. It is a perfect, a complete redemption. It is not a beggarly redemption, but a vast, God-sized redemption that glorifies God and glorifies Christ and honors every man who embraces it.

God *"has delivered us from the power of darkness"* (Colossians 1:13). That dark power is Satan's authority. If we are delivered out of his authority, he can no longer reign over us.

Yet the great body of the church is living under the dominion of the adversary as though it had never been born again. What is the matter? The creed to which we have subscribed has no actual redemption in it. It has robbed the church of its own redemption by setting stakes of limitation.

God delivered us out of the authority of darkness, the authority of Satan, "*and conveyed us into the kingdom of the Son of His love*" (Colossians 1:13).

Put that in the first person. *You* are the one who has been delivered. You are the one who has been placed into God's kingdom and family. In Christ, you have your redemption, the remission of everything that you ever did. It gives you the nature of God and takes out of you the nature of the adversary.

The new birth settles the problem of your sin nature. All you ever did is wiped out. All you ever were has been destroyed. You are now an actual child of God just as Jesus was in His earth walk. You have the same standing that Jesus had because Jesus is your standing. He has become your righteousness. God Himself becomes your standing.

> *With a view to demonstrating, at the present time, His righteousness, that He may be shown to be righteous Himself, and the giver of righteousness to those who believe in Jesus.*
> (Romans 3:26 WNT)

You have faith in Jesus as your substitute. So God has become your righteousness. When you believe this, you will come out of bondage, weakness, and failure into the fullness of this new life in Christ. You are the sons of God. You are heirs of God and joint heirs with Jesus Christ. You are redeemed. "*For you were bought at a price*" (1 Corinthians 6:20). That price was the blood of Christ.

Why do we become the slaves of wrong teaching, the slaves of sense knowledge? There is no joint ownership between Christ and the world. You either belong to the devil or you belong to Christ. Christ purchased you with His own blood.

> *Knowing that you were not redeemed with corruptible things, like silver or gold, from your aimless conduct received by tradition from your fathers, but with the precious blood of Christ,*

as of a lamb without blemish and without spot.
(1 Peter 1:18–19)

It is the blood of the spotless Lamb. You stand before the Father now a redeemed one, without condemnation. The blood of Jesus Christ, God's Son, redeemed you. Every claim of justice has been paid. Jesus met the demands of justice and satisfied them. You are free.

"Do not become slaves of men" (1 Corinthians 7:23). That means that we are not to become the servants of the theories of men or the creeds of men. *Men* here means the man who walks in the senses. You crown Jesus as the Lord of your life. There is no other bondage but the bondage of love.

And *"if the Son makes you free, you shall be free indeed"* (John 8:36). You are free from Satan's dominion. You are a new creation, a child of God. You have been redeemed from the hand of your enemy. You are to take this fact seriously. You are to order your life accordingly.

"Sin shall not have dominion over you" (Romans 6:14). Satan was defeated by your Master. That defeat stripped him of his ability to take you captive without your cooperation.

The two phases of Christ's ministry in redemption are:

1. Jesus paying the price of your redemption.
2. Jesus defeating your enemy and setting you free.

Having disarmed principalities and powers, He made a public spectacle of them, triumphing over them in it.
(Colossians 2:15)

Christ triumphed over the adversary. He defeated the enemy. His triumph was your triumph. That battle was your battle. He was not fighting for Himself.

> *Inasmuch then as the children have partaken of flesh and blood, He Himself likewise shared in the same, that through death He might destroy him who had the power of death, that is, the devil.* (Hebrews 2:14)

He set you free. You are free. You are redeemed by God Himself.

Next, I want you to notice that you are a new creation. This truth has never been given its place. All we have been taught was that God forgave us our sins and by a second work of grace, sin was eradicated from us.

But if we did wrong ignorantly or knowingly, we had to be justified again. That justification permitted us to be justified with the devil's nature in us.

Another view is that God was unable to take out Satan's nature when He gave us His nature, so that when we were born again, we had God's nature and the devil's nature in us. We warred against the old nature in us. They said we would be free when we died. But Satan is the author of death, so that would make Satan your savior. Far be the thought!

All this teaching belongs to sense knowledge's interpretation of the Word.

Spiritual things are spiritually understood. First Corinthians 2:12 says, *"That we might know the things that have been freely given to us by God."* The first thing that is given to you after redemption is a new nature.

Second Corinthians 5:17–18 must ever stand as the key to this wonderful truth:

> *Therefore, if anyone is in Christ, he is a new creation; old things have passed away; behold, all things have become new. Now all things are of God, who has reconciled us to Himself through Jesus Christ, and has given us the ministry of reconciliation.*

God was in Christ reconciling the world to Himself. You are reconciled to the Father. You are brought into fellowship with the Father. You are a new creation. The devil's nature has been taken out of you, and God's nature has taken its place.

Everything you were before stopped being. All you were in Satan stopped being. The old things of weakness and failure are passed. This new creation has no memory of the past creation. You are newly born. You are a new species. You are a new creation in Christ Jesus.

The Jew was blood-covered because his nature was antagonistic toward God. We are not blood-covered. We are made new creations. We are cleansed by the blood of Jesus. We need not be covered. We can stand free of sin consciousness in His presence just as Jesus did in His earth walk.

The Holy Spirit has given birth to us. We are born of God.

Of His own will He brought us forth by the word of truth, that we might be a kind of firstfruits of His creatures.
(James 1:18)

First John 4:4 says, "*You are of God, little children.*" We are God's "*workmanship, created in Christ Jesus*" (Ephesians 2:10).

All this drives us to the conclusion that this new creation is something that God Himself has wrought, and we are just what He says we are—the very sons of God.

Romans 6:6 tells us that the man of sin is done away in the new creation: "*Our old man was crucified with Him, that the body of sin might be done away with, that we should no longer be slaves of sin.*" The sin nature is gone.

So many of us have tried to get rid of this old nature. We did not know that it was put away.

The thing called the Adamic nature is spiritual death, which has possession of our spirits. When we are made alive, made new creations, that nature is done away.

We are tempted and in our babyhood state, we do foolish things. That is because our bodies have never yet been brought into subjection to our spirits. Desire may dwell in your physical body, but it is not sin until you have consented to an act that is forbidden in the Word.

There is nothing wrong in your body. Sin lived in your spirit and in your mind. It does not abide in your body.

When Romans 8:3 says God *"condemned sin in the flesh,"* this refers to sin in the senses. It is when your senses have gained the dominion over your spirit and mind.

> *I beseech you therefore, brethren, by the mercies of God, that you present your bodies a living sacrifice, holy, acceptable to God, which is your reasonable service. And do not be conformed to this world, but be transformed by the renewing of your mind, that you may prove what is that good and acceptable and perfect will of God.* (Romans 12:1–2)

God desires that these senses be dedicated to Him after we are born again. It is an unseemly thing for your senses to rule your mind and your spirit. You know that if you have a sore foot, that foot rules all the rest of your body. That disease has gained the mastery so that your spirit and your mind become absolute slaves to the pain in the foot.

The same thing is true if you have an unclean appetite, a habit. That habit gains the mastery over your whole being if you do not hold it in subjection.

The thing you should say to that foot is, "By His stripes, you are healed. In the name of Jesus, become well." (See Isaiah 53.)

You say to the habit that has gained the mastery over your body and mind, "You have no right to hold dominion over me any longer. In the name of Jesus Christ, depart." You will be free.

There is only one place for sin to actually reside, and that is in our spirits.

Our spirits have been recreated. The sin nature has been taken out. *"We know that we have passed from death to life, because we love the brethren"* (1 John 3:14). Satan's nature is gone. God's nature is in us. This new creation is of God. We know that we are His own.

Nothing will cripple one so quickly as to deny this truth. Nothing will establish you and build your faith as quickly as to confess it. Confess it in your heart first. Confess it out loud in your room. Say it over and over again: "I am a child of God. I have God's nature. I am the righteousness of God in Christ."

Say it until the words become familiar to your spirit. Say it until your spirit and your words agree, until your whole being swings into harmony and into line with the Word of God.

That miraculous passage in Hebrews 5:13 says, *"For everyone who partakes only of milk is unskilled in the word of righteousness, for he is a babe."* They have never sounded the depths of righteousness. They do not know what it means to have God justify them and have a standing with the Father just like Jesus's standing.

They do not seem to grasp the significance of the reality of the new creation. That new creation is a part of God. It has partaken of God's nature. It has been made out of righteousness and holiness of truth.

The new creation is not a man-made thing. It is not a mental thing. It is a thing of God.

Just as the angel said in Luke 1:35, *"That Holy One who is to be born will be called the Son of God,"* the Holy Spirit has given birth to you, and you are one of the holy ones of God. You absolutely belong to the Father. You are now His very child. You can say, "My Father," and He whispers, "My child."

> *For you did not receive the spirit of bondage again to fear, but you received the Spirit of adoption by whom we cry out, "Abba, Father."* (Romans 8:15)

This is your continual confession of your relationship to Him and His to you. That will build faith into you. Romans 8:1 says, *"There is therefore now no condemnation to those who are in Christ Jesus."* God is your Father, your protector, your caretaker, and your Lord. You are in His family. Take your place. Play the part of a son.

Let the world hear your confession. Every time you confess your sonship rights and your sonship place, you defeat the adversary.

Sickness has no dominion over you. Disease has no dominion over you. Want, hunger, and need have no dominion over you. You are now in the family of plenty.

You are in the family where you lie down in green pastures, and you are led by streams of sweet water. Your soul is restored from calamity, fear, and doubt. Your fellowship and communion with Him is quiet and beautiful.

You are walking now in the paths of righteousness, taking advantage of your righteousness. You are doing the works of a righteous man. You are praying the prayers of a righteous man. *"The effective, fervent prayer of a righteous man avails much"* (James 5:16).

You are praying for the sick. You are casting out demons. You are living a life of victory because you are the righteousness of God in Christ.

This in part is what eternal life gives us in Christ.

29

WHAT IS THE MATTER?

This man came to me, discouraged and disheartened.

I asked him, "What has happened?" He then related the following experience:

"The first few weeks after I received eternal life, I was floating through azure skies. It seemed that nothing could ever touch me, that I could never go back to the old life again. Then one day I received a fearful jar; things happened to me unexpectedly, and I found myself in darkness. The light had gone. All my joy seeped out. I did not know what to do. For days, I have lived in misery. I have come over to see you this morning to ask you what is the matter."

I said to him, "It is the simplest thing in the world. You have broken fellowship with your Father. You see, when you received eternal life, no one instructed you or told you what to do. You did not know exactly what you had received or how to take care of the thing that had been given to you.

"I passed through that myself. What you should have done when you received eternal life was to begin to study the Word. Our books and Bible study courses are what you need. They will teach you what you should know.

"Here is what has happened to you: Your fellowship has been broken. The adversary has taken advantage of you, and you have thought that you were never born again."

"Yes," he replied, "that is true. I remember that somebody said to me, 'If you had received eternal life, you would never have done that thing; you would never have said that thing.' I had no answer."

I told him, "I can understand that. I think that every believer goes through that experience unless he has been correctly instructed at the beginning. You should have known that you had been born into His family, that God was now your Father, that you were His child, that Jesus was your Intercessor ever living to pray for you, and that He is your Advocate at the right hand of the Father. You should have known 1 John 1:9: *If we confess our sins, He is faithful and just to forgive us our sins and to cleanse us from all unrighteousness.*"

He asked, "Well, what does that mean?"

I said, "It means that after you have received eternal life, if you do anything to break your fellowship with the Father and your heart feels desperate and miserable as a result of it, you should look up and say, 'Father, forgive me, I did not mean to say that.' The instant you confess your sins, He forgives you. You should have known 1 John 2:1: *My little children, these things I write to you, so that you may not sin. And if anyone sins, we have an Advocate with the Father, Jesus Christ the righteous.*"

I explained, "The moment you sinned, you lost your sense of righteousness. Fear took its place. Had you known that you had a righteous Advocate who could go into the Father's presence and plead your case for you, it would have saved you those days of misery. The next time anything happens, look up and say, 'Father, in Jesus's name, forgive me.' Then your Advocate takes the case over. You are forgiven."

He was relieved. "I thought I didn't have eternal life. I thought the whole thing had gone to pieces."

I said to him, "Well, it hasn't. You are still His child. I wonder if you know 1 John 5:13, *'These things I have written to you who believe in the name of the Son of God, that you may know that you have eternal life.'*"

He said, "I remember reading that Scripture, but I guess it didn't register at the time. I see it now. I have this eternal life in me now. Satan cannot take it from me. He cannot rob me of it. I am the Father's child. After I received eternal life, I asked the Holy Spirit to come and make His home in me. There is a passage somewhere that says, *'He who is in you is greater than he who is in the world.'*"

He was quoting from 1 John 4:4. I asked him, "Did you notice the first part of that verse? *'You are of God, little children, and have overcome them.'* We are of God. We are born from above. We have received the nature and life of our own Father God."

The discouraged man saw his rights in Christ. He said, "I want to thank you for this. You certainly have put me on my feet again. I'm going to take that Bible study course. I am going to know the Word. I am going to know my Father. Goodbye, and God bless you."

We are not just adopted into God's family. We haven't simply received forgiveness of our past sins. We have something infinitely more than that. All that we have ever done has been remitted—wiped out. That is called remission. When we received eternal life, we were made alive in Christ. The thing that had held us in bondage was spiritual death, the nature of the adversary.

That nature was driven out of us and the nature of the Father took its place. So we became new creations. Now all the temptations that come to us must come from without. They cannot come from within. And anything that comes to us from without can be conquered because greater is He who is in us than anything outside attempting to destroy us.

> *For whatever is born of God overcomes the world. And this is the victory that has overcome the world—our faith. Who is he who overcomes the world, but he who believes that Jesus is the Son of God?* (1 John 5:4–5)

It was faith in Jesus Christ when you accepted Him as Savior that brought you into the overcoming class. You are now an overcomer. You are now a conqueror. He has made you that.

In Romans 8:35–39, the Spirit enumerates all the things that can come against a believer. He climaxes it by saying, *"Yet in all these things we are more than conquerors through Him who loved us"* (verse 37).

No one can separate you from the love of God in Christ. They cannot do it. The Father loves you more now than He did before you were a Christian. And Jesus loves you more than He did before He died for you.

It was and is God's battle. It wasn't your battle then, and it is not your battle today.

> *Fear not, for I am with you; be not dismayed, for I am your God. I will strengthen you, yes, I will help you, I will uphold you with My righteous right hand.* (Isaiah 41:10)

Study this Scripture and meditate on it until every phrase of it becomes a part of you. *"Fear not"* means "do not look around you." Look at Him, look at the Word. Just keep your eyes on that Scripture. God is in that Word. He is behind it. He is behind you, and He will back you up to the limit.

Romans 8:31 is yours: *"If God is for us, who can be against us?"* God is for you. There aren't enough forces this side of hell to conquer you.

Satan can rob us of our fellowship with the Father, with the Word, with the brethren, and with ourselves, but he cannot rob us of our relationship with the Father.

30

THE UNBELIEVING BELIEVER

Here is a possessor of eternal life, yet he lives as though the Word were a fable. He has the living Word of God committed to memory but it is not a part of his life. He has never gone any further than sense knowledge faith carries him. He has become an assenter rather than a believer.

God calls him "son" and the Word calls him a believer, yet he does not enjoy his rights in Christ.

You know that John 6:47 (RSV) says, "*He who believes has eternal life.*" The believer, then, is a possessor, but this possessor is continually begging the Father to give him what already is his own.

John 1:16 says, "*And of His fullness we have all received, and grace for grace.*" The unbelieving believer has God's fullness of grace, and yet he is empty. He has His fullness of love, yet his senses dominate him. He has the riches of His grace, and yet he lives in the conscious sense of unworthiness, unfaithfulness, and lack.

This type of people is a continual source of sorrow to the heart of the man who is seeking to lead men into an enjoyment of their rights and privileges. What must it be to the heart of the Father! This person is one who has received the fullness of God, but who talks continually about his emptiness. His confession robs him of the joy.

> *Now to Him who is able to do exceedingly abundantly above all that we ask or think, according to the power that works in us.* (Ephesians 3:20)

God's ability is in him, yet he is talking about his lack of ability. He prays for faith. He prays for power. He has ability. God has given him all things, but he does not act on the Word.

THE ONE WHO LACKS

Let us consider for a moment the fact that here is God's ability to do *"exceedingly abundantly above all that we ask or think."* The ability of God is energizing in us right now.

The one who is talking about his lack has the ability of God within him. The house is wired. The bulbs are in their sockets. Everything is waiting for him to turn on the switch, yet he gropes in darkness. It is not a lack on the part of the Father. It is this man's lack of taking advantage of God's ability that is given to him that he may grow in grace, in knowledge, and in usefulness.

The abilities of God will increase in you.

You remember in the book of Acts: *"Then the word of God spread, and the number of the disciples multiplied greatly in Jerusalem"* (Acts 6:7). Then later, *"So the word of the Lord grew mightily and prevailed"* (Acts 19:20).

As you use the Word, it grows on you; it multiplies. After a while, it gains the ascendancy and controls you. It prevails against sense knowledge. It makes you a dominant person where you were a servant before. You become master of circumstances where you have led a cripple's life.

I saw one who had been locked in his chair for years. His legs refuse to bear the weight of his body. He is no more a prisoner than many of us who read this. The only difference is that his is a physical bondage, and yours is a spiritual one.

You are held in bondage to your mind. "I can't do it," you say. Your mind is under the dominion of your physical body, and your sense-ruled mind shrinks from giving God absolute control of your life.

"*Do you not know that your body is the temple of the Holy Spirit?*" (1 Corinthians 6:19). These senses of yours could become missionaries of love for Him if they were brought under the domination of the Word.

THE ONE IN BONDAGE

What good is eternal life in us if we do not give it full sway?

Here is one who is redeemed confessing his bondage. I say to him, "Do you believe Colossians 1:13–14?"

"Oh, yes," he replies, "I believe every word from Genesis to Revelation."

I say, "Hear this then: '*He has delivered us from the power of darkness and conveyed us into the kingdom of the Son of His love, in whom we have redemption through His blood, the forgiveness of sins.*' Is that true, brother?"

"Oh, yes," he says.

"Well, then you are not in bondage, are you? You've taken advantage of your rights, and you are reveling in the ability of God that has taken you out of the realm of darkness and has placed you in the realm of the lordship of Christ, where every need is met, where the ability of God is at your disposal."

He says, "Oh, no! I haven't faith for that."

I say, "But did you notice that the word *faith* did not occur here? He says He has delivered you out of the authority of darkness and that you are now in the realm of the Son of His love, and that in Him, you have your redemption. It is not a problem of faith. It required faith to get into God's family, but you are now in it. You are what He says you are. He says you are free. He says you are in the kingdom of the Son of His love and you are redeemed. Darkness and Satan have no dominion over you."

A look of confusion fills the face of my friend. "I don't just understand this," he says.

I say to him, "Here is your difficulty: You have assented to the Scripture, but you have not acted on it. You've never said to yourself and your loved ones, 'I am free. I have been delivered out of the hand and authority of Satan. The life of God in me is stronger than the forces of darkness that surround me. You have never said it to yourself. Now say with confidence: 'From this day, I am a master of the forces of darkness because the life of God, the ability of God, and the wisdom of God are all mine.'"

He says, "Tell me how to act on the Word in my daily life."

I ask him, "Is it absolutely true what I have read? Then praise the Father and thank Him that you see your freedom at last and you are going to walk in it. From now on, you are what He says you are, and you have what He says you have. You can do what He says you can do because His enabling ability is in you."

He says, "That is a faith walk."

I say, "Yes, but we don't call it a faith walk. We just simply act on the Word. If we act on the Word, it becomes real. It never becomes real until you begin to practice it. That helpless invalid never enjoyed freedom from sickness until he acted on the Word of Jesus. The Master said, 'Arise, take up thy bed and walk.' And the man acted on what Jesus said. Now you begin to act on what Jesus says to you, and you will no longer be barren or unfruitful."

THE UNWORTHY ONE

Another who has become the righteousness of God in Christ is confessing his unworthiness and lack of ability to stand in the Father's presence without the sense of sin consciousness.

Romans 3:22 declares that there is a righteousness of God available on the ground of faith in Jesus Christ, and it belongs to all who believe. That is, every believer has a right to act and walk as a righteous one.

In Romans 3:26 (WNT), we read, "*With a view to demonstrating, at the present time, His righteousness, that He may be shown to be righteous Himself, and the giver of righteousness to those who believe in Jesus.*"

You have faith in Jesus. You have taken Him as your Savior. You have confessed Him as your Lord. You know that God raised Him from the dead. He was delivered up on account of your trespasses, and He was raised when you were declared righteous by God.

Now the Father dares to say to you, "As you have taken My Son as your Savior and have acknowledged His lordship, I voluntarily become your righteousness." Righteousness here means freedom from sin consciousness, a legal right to stand in the Father's presence without the sense of guilt or inferiority, to stand as a very son.

You remember 2 Corinthians 5:21: "*He made Him who knew no sin to be sin for us, that we might become the righteousness of God in Him.*" This is what He says about you, and you should never challenge the integrity of what God did in Christ for you by talking about being unworthy, unrighteous, or unfit after He has made you His righteousness.

Notice these facts:

- He made you alive in Christ Jesus.

- He made you the righteousness of God in Christ Jesus.
- He made you to be His own son, a partaker of His own nature.
- He has also made you a joint heir with Jesus.

He has made you all this in the new creation. This is what eternal life has done for you. This is what you actually are.

Now joy will come to you when you begin to praise the Father for what He is to you and for what you are to Him. You will begin to enjoy the fullness of this life when you begin to do what He enables you to do and take your place as a son in His family.

A father may love a sickly crippled son, but the crippled condition is a grief to him. Our heavenly Father may love us though we are in a crippled, weakened, Satan-ruled condition, but it robs Him of the joy that belongs to Him.

THE UNWISE SON

Think of the pathetic picture of one who has Christ as his wisdom living in poverty of spirit and continually confessing his lack of ability. Yet the Father said through Paul that He made Jesus to be wisdom unto us.

James, you remember, tells us to ask for wisdom if we lack it. (See James 1:5.) But James is writing to the babe in Christ, the man who is ruled by his senses, the man who has never enjoyed his fullness in Christ.

The Father, however, is speaking to us through Paul when He says, "Son, I am giving the wisdom that was manifested in Jesus's ministry to you. You will remember that when My Son was here, He faced every circumstance that confronted Him as a Master. He confused His enemies, who were inspired by the devil. I'm giving the wisdom that He had to you. It is yours.

"His wisdom, then, is imparted to you through the Word, for this Word is My wisdom. If you will feed on it, meditate in it, act on it, you need have no worry about mistakes or failures. You have My nature in you. I have imparted Myself to your spirit. I have not only imparted My love and Myself, but I've imparted My wisdom to your spirit. If you will listen to your spirit and follow it, the adversary can never take advantage of you.

"Your spirit is like Me. I never sleep. Your spirit never sleeps. Your spirit never grows old. It never has any of the infirmities of old age. It is not like a battery that can run down and need to be recharged. It always possesses the fullness of light, joy, liberty, and My very ability.

"But you must remember what Jesus said in Matthew 4:4: 'Man shall not live by bread alone, but by every word that proceeds from the mouth of God.' Your spirit cannot feed on sense knowledge, the literature of the day; it only feeds upon My Word. Your sense-ruled mind may feed upon novels and the literature of the day, but since you are recreated and have My life in your spirit, your spirit demands the bread of heaven."

THE SICK ONE

Here is one filled with sickness and disease. That disease was laid on Christ and yet he is crying continually to Him to heal him.

The other day, I read Isaiah 53:4 (YLT) to him:

Surely our sicknesses he hath borne, And our pains—he hath carried them, And we—we have esteemed him plagued, Smitten of God, and afflicted [with my diseases]. *And he is pierced for our transgressions, Bruised for our iniquities, The chastisement of our peace* [is] *on him, And by his bruise* [or His stripes] *there is healing to us.*

This is the great substitutionary chapter. You will notice that before He deals with the sin problem, He deals with the disease problem. Notice carefully that both disease and sin are spiritual.

Physical disease is a spiritual infirmity. This man whose body is filled with disease does not realize that those diseases were laid upon Jesus, that He suffered the pains of them, and that He put them away with his sins.

This man who is healed—in the mind of the Father, according to the testimony of Jesus, and according to the Word—is crying to the Father for his healing.

He is like the others who are the fullness of God, who are new creations in Christ, who have all the ability of God and yet live in weakness and failure. This man whose diseases made Jesus sick and sent Him to the place of suffering has never yet seen the reality of that Scripture. He acts as though Jesus had never borne his diseases.

THE HABIT SLAVE

Here is a man who has been under the bondage of drink and held an absolute slave to that demon for years. When he awakens after a debauch, he says, "I wish I could get my deliverance from this habit."

And yet Jesus delivered him. In the mind of the Father, he is delivered but he doesn't know it. He drinks again and again. He talks just as unwisely as the other man did.

Both of them are redeemed from the power of the adversary, but they do not act on the Word. Neither of them is taking advantage of the things God wrought in Christ for him. Both live in defeat, pain, and misery when health and deliverance belong to them.

You remember this passage from 1 Kings 18:21: *"How long will you falter between two opinions? If the* Lord *is God, follow Him; but if Baal, follow him."* If these two who are drunken with their misery and halting between the two sides would act on the Word, they would find their immediate deliverance. Both are delivered and have Christ's strength but are confessing their weakness.

THE AVERAGE BELIEVER

Here is a sorry picture, an unhappy one. It is a denial of the Word. It is a confession of Satan's supremacy. It is the affirmation of weakness. It is a subtle inspiration from the adversary that declares that God is a liar.

The average believer wouldn't admit it if you asked him. He says, "I am in Him. I am in Christ. I know that I am a new creation. I know that I have eternal life, but I can't conquer this. I can't overcome that. I'm so weak. I just live in bondage. I can't rise above my circumstances."

Such Christians do not know that God delivered them out of the realm of darkness where they were living and translated them into the kingdom of the Son of His love. In Him, they have their redemption from all these things that they are suffering now. In the mind of the Father, they are redeemed. Not only are they redeemed, but they are masters where they once served as slaves.

Psalm 27:1 says, "*The Lord is my light and my salvation; whom shall I fear? The Lord is the strength of my life; of whom shall I be afraid?*" That was not written to Israel. This is a new creation truth. Here is salvation and light. There is no reason why you should ever walk in darkness again.

HE IS THE LIGHT OF LIFE

Jesus is the light of life, and that life is eternal life. The eternal life that you have received has in it the light, the wisdom, and the ability of God. It is now the very strength of your life.

You have God's ability and God's strength. You needn't be afraid of anybody or anything. He is the very strength of your physical body, your mind, and your spirit.

You see, it wouldn't honor the Father to have a family of weaklings. It wouldn't glorify Him to have His children held in bondage by the adversary. He wants His children free—and He has set them free.

Now you can see what eternal life does for a man. You can see that eternal life is the nature of the Father. When it gains control of our sense-ruled minds, it can lead us out of any weakness, any condition, or any circumstances where we have been held in captivity into the very light and life of Christ.

Every believer is a master in the mind of the Father. We are God's men. We are the new creation folks, and it is a disgrace to heaven to have us wallow in weakness, failure, and lack.

Let us say now, "I am what God says I am."

31

A NEW TYPE OF CHRISTIANITY

Discerning men and women have been asking for a new type of Christianity. They do not want a new philosophy or a new metaphysical concept of Christ, but an unveiling of the reality that was seen in Jesus in His earth walk.

We have looked behind for it, but it is not in the past. The early church did not have the thing for which hearts are craving.

You understand that the early church did not have the Pauline revelation of Christ, His substitution, the body of Christ, or His ministry at the right hand of the Father for us. They had the contact of the three years of Christ's earth walk. They were new creations; they had experienced all that God reveals to us through Paul, but they did not understand.

They knew of His death on the cross. They had seen it. They knew of His resurrection as a reality. They had eaten with Him, walked with Him, and fellowshipped with Him after His resurrection. They had seen Him ascend. They were present on the day of Pentecost when the Holy Spirit came to the earth, when the church was born.

However, they did not know that they were new creations. They had firsthand sense knowledge evidence of everything that took place, but they did not know they were the righteousness of God in Christ. They had marvelous experiences but did not know what caused it.

They were not walking by faith then. They were walking by sight, by hearing, and by feeling.

John's first epistle begins:

That which was from the beginning, which we have heard, which we have seen with our eyes, which we have looked upon, and our hands have handled, concerning the Word of life.

(1 John 1:1)

The early church walked in the realm of the senses. God permitted it because the fuller revelation had not been given. The Pauline revelation did not get into the hands of the church until after the beginning of the second century.

WHAT IS THIS NEW THING?

Paul's revelation was the new man created in Christ Jesus. "*If anyone is in Christ, he is a new creation*" (2 Corinthians 5:17). This new man will be like Christ. "*For we are His workmanship, created in Christ Jesus*" (Ephesians 2:10). In his love life, the new man carries the solution of the human problem. He will bring God to the earth again. He will live and walk as Jesus lived and walked among men.

Here are some striking facts about this new creation man.

You shall know the truth, and the truth shall make you free. ... Therefore if the Son makes you free, you shall be free indeed. (John 8:32, 36)

You shall know the reality, and that reality shall set you free. What is this reality? It is the answer to the human heart's craving. It is the thing for which man through the ages has been searching. This heart hunger has given all the human religions to us.

This new man who comes into the full consciousness of his rights will be free.

Colossians 1:9 has some startling truths: *"For this reason we also, since the day we heard it, do not cease to pray for you, and to ask that you may be filled with the knowledge of His will in all wisdom and spiritual understanding."*

This is the prayer that the Spirit has prayed for every one of us: *"That you may be filled with the knowledge of His will in all wisdom and spiritual understanding."* The Greek word *epiginosko*, which is translated "knowledge," is more than simply knowledge. It is exact knowledge, perfect knowledge. It is a knowledge in all spiritual wisdom and revelation.

Spiritual wisdom is not a product of the senses, for sense knowledge cannot fathom it. For instance, the first three chapters in Ephesians are an example of the use of *epiginosko*. They let down the curtain so that we may look into the very purpose of the heart of the Father God.

This knowledge is a knowledge of His will. He never willed that we should be toys in the hand of the enemy. He planned that when the church came into being, it would be composed of His sons and daughters, who would be demon masters and world rulers. They were to rule the laws of nature. They were to dominate the laws of nature as Jesus did in His earth walk. They were to control the winds and the waves. They were to be masters of the animal creation. In the name of Jesus, they were to have the lost authority of the garden of Eden restored to them.

But the church does not know anything about it. We have been taught that we are poor, weak worms of the dust, that we must be ruled by Satan, that we must live lives of poverty and want, and that we are too unworthy to have our prayers answered. They have cultivated in us a sense of unworthiness that has robbed us of spiritual initiative and kept us in a state of bondage to fear, ignorance, and sin.

We did not know the sin problem had been settled. The object of this knowledge is so that *"you may walk worthy of the Lord, fully pleasing Him, being fruitful in every good work and increasing in the knowledge of God"* (Colossians 1:10).

Jesus said He is the vine, and we are His branches. We are a part of Christ. We are a shoot out of Christ, and Christ's fruit is to be borne by us. He cannot bear fruit now. We are the branches, so we are to bear fruit in every good work. Meanwhile we are increasing in this exact knowledge of the Father. We are to be *"strengthened with all might, according to His glorious power, for all patience and longsuffering with joy"* (Colossians 1:11).

That is climactic! That is lifting us above circumstances, above the dominion and power of Satan, and making us absolute masters where we have tremblingly served as slaves.

We have the solution to this in the 12th verse: *"Giving thanks to the Father who has qualified us to be partakers of the inheritance of the saints in the light."*

WE ARE REDEEMED

We have been delivered out of the authority of Satan. Satan no longer has a right to rule over us. The church has never acknowledged it, has never known it. Here and there, an individual has entered into his inheritance, but the rank and file of the church have lived under the bondage of fear and doubt and satanic supremacy.

We are not only delivered out of Satan's dominion, but we are taken *"into the kingdom of the Son of His love"* (Colossians 1:13). This is the new creation. This is where the sons of God actually *"reign as kings in Life through the one individual, Jesus Christ"* (Romans 5:17 WNT).

It is in Christ that we have our redemption, the remission of all that we have ever done. We have been redeemed out of the hand of the enemy. We have been recreated. We have received the nature and life of the Deity.

We have come into the family of God, and as sons and daughters, we are enjoying the fellowship of our Father. We are exercising our rights and privileges in the name of Jesus. Disease and sickness have lost their dominion. We are masters over them. Poverty and want no longer challenge us. We know our Father.

The church has been dominated by sense knowledge, which has given it the sense of unworthiness. How many times we have said, "If I could live a holy life, a pure life, a Jesus life, I would have the same ability that Jesus had."

How men everywhere have hunted for holy men who could do their praying for them! The sick are continually searching for someone who can pray the prayer of faith while they live in the realm of unbelief.

They do not know that as sure as they were born again, they became new creations and received the very nature of the Father God. That nature has made their spirits whole. That nature has made them new creations. The sin problem has been settled for them. They are now the righteousness of God in Christ. They can stand in the Father's presence just as Jesus did, but they do not know it.

They can have their prayers answered as Jesus did, but they do not understand it. They have lived in ignorance of spiritual things.

They have much sense knowledge. They have all that our schools and colleges and universities can impart and yet that sense knowledge has not unveiled to them what they are in Christ. They do not know that they have as much a right in the Father's presence as Jesus has, so that with all boldness, they may stand before that throne of grace unabashed, without sin consciousness. If they knew these things, fear would no longer dominate them. They would be masters. They would no longer submit to the rule of the senses.

LORDSHIP OF THE WORD

If this knowledge could only be given to them, they would pass over into the love realm. They would joyfully admit the lordship of the Word. They would begin to live the love life.

Now they are afraid of it. They do not know that Jesus brought a new kind of love that was a part of God Himself. *"God is love"* (1 John 4:8), and this new kind of love has been given to us.

This is the genius of Christianity. This new kind of life and this new kind of love beget a new kind of righteousness—a righteousness that cannot be obtained by works, by sacrifice, by prayer, or by anything else a man can do. It is a gift that comes with the new creation. Every child of God has it.

Until a man knows that he is the righteousness of God, he will never take advantage of his privileges. He will always live in bondage to the enemy. But the instant he knows it, he will come boldly into the presence of the Father. He will feel at home in the throne room.

I want you to note John 1:16: *"And of His fullness we have all received, and grace for grace."*

This new creation is the fullness of God as we are taught in Ephesians 1:22–23: *"And He put all things under His feet, and gave Him to be head over all things to the church, which is His body, the fullness of Him who fills all in all."* Fullness means completeness.

Christ's nature and life have been poured into our spirits. Where we were empty and had only a vague longing in life, we now have found reality.

EQUIPPED OF GOD

This new creation, this new type of Christianity, is equipped of God for a supernatural life. God furnishes the equipment.

In Ephesians 6:11–12, He says:

Put on the whole armor of God, that you may be able to stand against the wiles of the devil. For we do not wrestle against flesh and blood, but against principalities, against powers, against the rulers of the darkness of this age, against spiritual hosts of wickedness in the heavenly places.

Our combat is not a mental one, nor a physical one. It is a spiritual combat. No spiritual combat is fought by physical self-denial or a mental struggle. A spiritual battle is not won by physical means, mental means, or any kind of work that a man can do. The battle has already been fought by Jesus and won. We do not fight in this battle.

THIS IS A FAITH FIGHT

We win our battle by our recognition that it has already been fought and won by Jesus and by accepting the thing that Jesus has done for us. We do not pray for it. We do not struggle for it. We simply look up and say, "Father, I thank You that the battle has been won."

In the faith fight, God does it all. He conquered Satan and put away sin. He bore our diseases, so that we only need to thank Him and enjoy it.

Stand therefore, having girded your waist with truth, having put on the breastplate of righteousness, and having shod your feet with the preparation of the gospel of peace; above all, taking the shield of faith with which you will be able to quench all the fiery darts of the wicked one. And take the helmet of salvation, and the sword of the Spirit, which is the word of God. (Ephesians 6:14–17)

We stand in that evil day when the temptations come like a flood, having girded our loins with this truth or reality. We have come to know the reality of the finished work of Christ.

We put on the breastplate of righteousness. We act it, use it, and confess it. We know that we are the righteousness of God in Him. This is an acknowledged fact. We know what we are in Him. We know that righteousness permits us to stand in the Father's presence without the sense of guilt or inferiority.

Our feet have been shod with the preparation of the good tidings of peace. We can run now with a message of peace to the world. We can bring to men the good tidings.

And we have the shield of faith that withstands all the fiery darts of the evil one.

SPIRITUAL FORCES STRONGER THAN PHYSICAL

God is a Spirit. He created man so He can create new flesh where disease has destroyed it.

God created this world of ours, filled it with rocks and all these physical objects by just the word of faith. This word of faith can rebuild destroyed tissues in our bodies.

You can understand that our combat is not with physical things, but with spiritual things. Our enemies are spirits. The diseases that afflict men are spiritual.

When our reasoning faculties are convinced of these realities, disease is defeated.

The ills that afflict men are spiritual ones. We are masters of those things. In the name of Jesus, we reign as kings. We take *"the helmet of salvation, and the sword of the Spirit, which is the word of God"* (Ephesians 6:17).

The combat is fought with our lips. On our lips is the Word of God, which is the sword of the Spirit. With that Word, we conquer disease. We say, "Disease, in the name of Jesus Christ, stop being. Cancer, in the name of Jesus, shrivel up and stop being. Tuberculosis, in the name of Jesus, leave that body." We are masters. He made us masters. He made us to rule them as He did in His earth walk.

> *Praying always with all prayer and supplication in the Spirit, being watchful to this end with all perseverance and supplication for all the saints.* (Ephesians 6:18)

> *Not that we are sufficient of ourselves to think of anything as being from ourselves, but our sufficiency is from God, who also made us sufficient as ministers of the new covenant.*
> (2 Corinthians 3:5–6)

God has given to us His own sufficiency, His own ability. Take this Scripture as an illustration: *"Now to Him who is able to do exceedingly abundantly above all that we ask or think, according to the power* [or ability] *that works in us"* (Ephesians 3:20).

God's marvelous ability is at work within us. We are equipped by God and with God. We have His Word that created the universe. We have His Word that can slay or make alive. We have the name of Jesus, and all the authority of heaven is behind it and is invested in it. We have the power of attorney to use that name.

We have the great and mighty Holy Spirit who raised Jesus from the dead dwelling in us. We have the same ability at work within us that wrought in Christ in His earth walk.

Read carefully Ephesians 1:19–20. I want you to know the *"exceeding greatness"* of God's power *"toward us who believe."* It is according to the strength of His might *"which He worked in Christ when He raised Him from the dead."*

Our equipment is spiritual, and spiritual things are mightier than physical. The church has ability today to destroy the atheistic forces that seek to wipe out the effect of Christian civilization. The church does not know that it has His ability. The church is utterly ignorant of her place in the purpose of God.

Wars are created by demons, carried on by demon inspiration, but the church is the master of demons. First John 4:4 says, *"You are of God, little children, and have overcome them, because He who is in you is greater than he who is in the world."* How little we have appreciated this!

The mighty Holy Spirit, who renewed the face of the earth, who healed the sick and raised the dead, and who hushed the sea through Christ, is the same Holy Spirit that we have today. He has lost none of His ability.

The Father has tried to tell us that this One in us is greater than the demonic forces of the earth. He says, "Greater is He that is in you than he that is in the world. You are masters. You are rulers. Demons cannot rule the world without your consent. I have given you all authority over all the power of the enemy. Now go and exercise it!"

"But of Him you are in Christ Jesus, who became for us wisdom from God" (1 Corinthians 1:30). Here Jesus is made unto us wisdom. It is God's wisdom, not man's. It is the wisdom that is greater than satanic wisdom.

TWO KINDS OF WISDOM

There are two kinds of wisdom spoken of in the Word. There is one that comes down from above and one that is of the earth, earthy, sensual, or demonic.

The one from above is the wisdom that Jesus exercised in His earth walk. It is the wisdom that Jesus, the Father, and the Holy Spirit used in creation. We have access to it.

Can't you see that we can defeat the adversary? Can't you see that no matter what plans he makes, we are his superiors? All that we need is to learn the secret of utilizing this wisdom.

We have been trusting in lawyers and doctors who have nothing but sense knowledge. We have ignored our right to this supreme wisdom.

John 8:12 adds more light on this subject: *"I am the light of the world. He who follows Me shall not walk in darkness, but have the light of life."* This means divine wisdom. This means that we are no longer to walk in doubt, fear, and uncertainty. We walk as Jesus did, with a sure step.

> *He who loves his brother abides in the light, and there is no cause for stumbling in him. But he who hates his brother is in darkness and walks in darkness, and does not know where he is going, because the darkness has blinded his eyes.*
> (1 John 2:10–11)

This is what eternal life does in us. Let us tell it to the world.

LAST WORDS

You have read the book. Please let our ministry know your reactions to this message and if you'd like to have a share in giving it to people. This knowledge places responsibility, and responsibility is a call from God.

We will be glad to have your fellowship in giving this message to clergy, students in Bible schools, colleges, theological institutions, Sunday school workers, and Christian laymen.

ABOUT THE AUTHOR

Dr. E. W. Kenyon (1867–1948) was born in Saratoga County, New York. At age nineteen, he preached his first sermon. He pastored several churches in New England and founded the Bethel Bible Institute in Spencer, Massachusetts. This school later became the Providence Bible Institute when it was relocated to Providence, Rhode Island.

Kenyon served as an evangelist for over twenty years. In 1931, he became a pioneer in Christian radio on the Pacific Coast with his show *Kenyon's Church of the Air*, for which he earned the moniker "The Faith Builder." He also began the New Covenant Baptist Church in Seattle.

In addition to his pastoral and radio ministries, Kenyon wrote extensively. Among his books are the Bible courses *The Bible in the Light of Our Redemption: From Genesis Through Revelation* and *Studies in the Deeper Life: A Scriptural Study of Great Christian Truths*, and more than twenty other works, including *The Two Kinds of Knowledge*, *The New Kind of Love*, *The Father and His Family*, *Jesus the Healer*, *In His Presence: The Secret of Prayer*, *The Blood Covenant*, and *Two Kinds of Righteousness*.

His words and works live on through Kenyon's Gospel Publishing Society. Please visit www.kenyons.org for more information.